A Celebration
of Birds

ROBERT DOUGALL

A Celebration
of Birds

Illustrated by John Barber

COLLINS AND HARVILL PRESS
London 1978

© Robert Dougall, 1978

ISBN 0 00 262113 4

Made and printed litho in Great Britain
by W & J Mackay Ltd, Chatham
for Collins, St James's Place,
and Harvill Press Ltd, 30A Pavilion Road,
London SW1

Contents

TO NAN
who really likes cats best

Preface

Yet another book on birds? Yes, but, I think, one with a difference. In no way is it intended for people whose interest is mainly scientific, but rather for those members of the general public who may perhaps be wondering just what it is that others enjoy in birdwatching.

My aim is simply to invite the reader to add an enrichment, a new dimension of interest, I might almost say a sixth sense to his or her life. Once awakened, however belatedly, it is an interest that seldom goes to sleep again: it can lend fresh charm to every country walk, to every wood or hedgerow; it can equally be enjoyed in town gardens or city parks.

I feel that perhaps my best qualification for writing this book is that, somehow, I contrived to spend the first thirty years of my life without having my eyes fully opened. For reasons of space I have limited myself to fourteen birds. Half of these can be seen around us daily almost anywhere in Britain, but with the help of imaginative, sensitive writings in verse and prose, which I have culled from many sources, I hope that they will now come more sharply into focus: that they may be seen with fresh eyes.

The remainder belong more to the country or the seashore and include those two birds which more than any others have represented triumphs for the Royal Society for the Protection of Birds – the return of the Osprey and of the Avocet. John Barber's illustrations, while ornithologically correct, have also exactly the quality I was seeking: his birds are individuals.

I am greatly indebted above all to Jean Bowden for her enthusiastic and knowledgeable research assistance, to Gerald Searle of the RSPB for kindly reading the material and to Niki Talbot, who surpassed even her impeccable standards in faultlessly and speedily typing the manuscript.

Robert Dougall

I

The Robin

On the face of it, there's little to connect a homely, confiding robin with a reptile. Yet, like the whole great family of birds, his ancestry can be traced back to a strange-looking creature about the size of a magpie, which combined the characteristics of bird and reptile and lived between 130 and 140 million years ago. We know it had well-developed feathers but the breastbone lacked a keel, so the flying muscles can only have been weak. On the curve of each wing were three claws, which must have helped it to clamber up to the top-most branches from which to launch itself into a glide from tree to tree. Unlike modern birds we know today, none of its bones was hollow. This extra weight would be another reason why it could only glide and not fly.

All this was deduced from the chance discovery of some fossils, when a slab of limestone was split asunder in a quarry in Bavaria in 1861. The imprint of feathers was unmistakable and, later that year, a skeleton was found. These remains were acquired by the Natural History Department of the British Museum and this exciting evolutionary link between the ancient reptiles and modern birds was given the awkward scientific name of *Archaeopteryx lithographica*.

It was exciting because so few birds ever become fossilised. In fact some people often wonder why, when there are so many millions of birds, are their corpses so seldom seen? What happens when a bird dies? The answer of course is that the remains are often eaten by scavengers or rapidly decompose. Sickly birds also make for thick cover and are therefore likely to die unseen. Their bodies are light and fragile and, in consequence, seldom preserved by fossilisation. An exception is when the remains fall into the deposits on the beds of slow-running rivers or into tranquil lakes and seas. In the case of *Archaeopteryx*, the slate in which the fossil was found had been formed from silt at the bottom of a lake.

I mention this because it's nice to start at the beginning, but my main fascination with wild birds is not primarily concerned with scientific study. I am happy simply to enjoy them as an important enrichment of life and one that many of us all too often take for granted.

A few years ago, I spent a holiday in early summer in northern Italy. The scenery was superb, the sun shone, but after a day or two I sensed a deadness in the air: there was no birdsong. It is the same in parts of south-west France, in Cyprus or in Malta, where grisly mass-destructions of migratory birds take place each spring and autumn. Those same songbirds, protected and fed at countless bird-tables in Britain and other parts of Europe, are massacred in millions by guns and trapped in nets or by the revolting use of bird-lime daubed on twigs. Tethered or caged birds are often used as decoys to entice and call down their fellow creatures to be slaughtered. Migrating flocks of robins, larks, warblers and other tiny birds are all considered fair game.

What a blessing that in Britain we have, at last, learnt to value and give protection to our songbirds – and just in time. Already, even many of our most common birds have lost their natural living-space: thousands of square miles of countryside have disappeared under concrete for motorways or development of one kind or another. On the farms tens of thousands of miles of ancient hedgerows have been grubbed out to make bigger fields for cumbersome and expensive agricultural machinery. For this reason, our gardens are now more important than ever in providing reasonably safe breeding-places for countless birds. There is also much we can do to help by regularly feeding them in winter and by putting up nesting-boxes. The provision of a pond or shallow bird-bath, even if it is only an inverted dustbin lid, is another essential, especially in hot, dry weather and it will of course give exceptional opportunities for observing garden birds with their defences down.

It is interesting that whenever a poll is taken to decide Britain's most popular bird, invariably, the robin comes out on top. He has probably always been the first favourite.

The Robin

In his *Ancient Lives of the Scottish Saints* L. M. Metcalfe recounts this charming little tale from the twelfth century of St Kentigern as a boy:

The fellow-pupils of St Kentigern, seeing that he was loved by their teacher . . . hated him. Now a little bird, which on account of the redness of its body is called the redbreast, was wont to receive its daily food from the hand of Serf the teacher, and had thus become familiar and at home with him. Sometimes it was wont even to rest upon his head, or face, or shoulder, or in his bosom, or to sit by his side as he prayed or read; and by the flapping of its wings or by the sound of its inarticulate voice . . . showed its affection.

On a certain day the boys took advantage of his absence to indulge in play with the aforesaid little bird; and, while they handled it among themselves, and tried to snatch it from each other, it died in their hands . . .

At length, having taken counsel among themselves, they laid the blame on the boy Kentigern, who had kept himself entirely aloof from the affair, thinking to lessen the grace of friendship which Serf had hitherto entertained towards him.

When Kentigern, that most pure child, heard this, he took the bird into his hands, put the head to the body, and impressed upon it the sign of the cross, and raising his pure hands in prayer to the Lord, said: 'O Lord Jesus Christ, in whose hands is the breath of all Thy creatures, give back to this little bird the breath of life, that Thy blessed name may be glorified for ever.' These words spake the Saint in prayer, and immediately the bird was restored to life; and not only rose safely with untrammelled flight into the air, but flew forth in its usual way to meet the old man with joy as he returned from the church.

Six centuries later, Wordsworth had no doubts himself about the popularity of the robin, when he put the question:

> Art thou the bird whom man loves best,
> The pious bird with the scarlet breast,
> Our little English robin?

Like most of our British songbirds the redbreast was originally confined to the great forests and woods that covered the land when the ice-age gradually retreated. These are the same species that have now adapted to town gardens. What they have lost in cover and freedom from disturbance they have gained in the comparative abundance of food in winter. I suspect that the robin may well have been one of the first birds to discover the benefits to be gained from an association with man. In Britain at least he certainly basks in a special relationship and believes in keeping a beady eye on all man's activities.

One of the great nineteenth-century naturalists the Rev. F. O. Morris wrote of him in *A History of British Birds*:

An inhabitant of the wildest wood and the gayest garden, the most frequented road, and the most retired lane, the edge of the pasture field, and the neighbourhood of every country-house, the Robin is an acquaintance of both old and young and to each and all he seems like an old friend. As you walk along the hedgerow side at almost any season of the year, your wandering thought is for a moment arrested by the sight of a red breast perched on one of the topmost sprays, or by the sound of the pretty note that its owner warbles before you: you cannot help but stop a moment and speak a word to the well-known bird, as if to an old companion, and you almost fancy from his winsome attitude, the attention he seems to pay, and the quietness with which he remains, that he understands, if not your language, yet the purport of it, and is aware that you are a friend who will not hurt or harm him.

Similarly, Richard Jefferies in his epic tale *Bevis* in which he relives the freedom of his boyhood days at Coate Farm in Wiltshire breaks off the narrative to comment:

The hazel bushes seemed quite vacant; only one bird passed while they were there, and that was a robin, come to see what they were doing, and if there was anything for him. In the butchery of the Wars of the Roses, that such flowers should be stained with such memories! It is certain that the murderers watched the robin perched hard by. He listened to the voice of fair Rosamond; he was at the tryst when Amy Robsart met her lover. Nothing happens in the fields and woods without a robin.

Certainly any gardener knows how true that is today. Nothing escapes his interest. He seems to need companionship and contact: leave the garden fork for a moment stuck in a flowerbed and there he will be in a trice blithely perching on the handle, while it's still warm.

Of course, much of his interest in the gardener is due to the worms and insects made available to him by the digging, and yet there seems more to it than that. Provided there are no cats about, a robin will make the friendliest approaches inside the house as well.

This is especially the case in the hard days of winter, as the Scottish poet James Thomson records in the first of his 'Seasons' written in 1726:

The fowls of heaven, tamed by the cruel season crowd around the winnowing store, and claim the little boon which Providence assigns them. One alone, the red-breast, sacred to the household gods, wisely regardful of the embroiling sky, in joyless fields and thorny thickets, leaves his shivering mates, and pays to trusted man his annual visit. Half afraid, he first against the window beats; then brisk alights on the warm hearth; then hopping o'er the floor, eyes all the smiling family askance, and pecks and starts and wonders where he is; till more familiar grown, the table crumbs attract his slender feet.

Years later Wordsworth observed how the robins came right into the Westmorland cottage where he lived with his wife and his beloved sister Dorothy. When she was ill one even stayed in her room:

Our cats having been banished the house, it was soon frequented by redbreasts. My sister being then confined to her room by sickness, as, dear creature, she still is, had one that, without being caged, took up its abode with her, and at night used to perch upon a nail from which a picture had hung. It used to sing and fan her face with its wings in a manner that was very touching.

William was so impressed that he wrote a poem about the incident from which I quote:

The Redbreast

Driven in by Autumn's sharpening air
From half-stripped woods and pastures bare,
Brisk Robin seeks a kindlier home:
Not like a beggar is he come,

> But enters as a looked-for guest,
> Confiding in his ruddy breast,
> As if it were a natural shield
> Charged with a blazon on the field,
> Due to that good and pious deed
> Of which we in the Ballad read.

And later in the poem, he refers to Dorothy:

> But small and fugitive our gain
> Compared with *hers* who long hath lain,
> With languid limbs and patient head
> Reposing on a lone sick-bed;
> Where now, she daily hears a strain
> That cheats her of too busy cares,
> Eases her pain and helps her prayers.

The naturalist W. T. Greene writing in 1885 remembered a railway robin:

I once saw a Robin in the refreshment-room of a country railway station, perched on a champagne bottle on the topmost shelf behind the bar; Whence, as soon as the coast was clear, he descended to pick up the crumbs left upon the counter, returning as soon as he had satisfied his appetite, to his coign of vantage, whence he gaily warbled a cheerful little song of thanksgiving. That was the second winter, the attendant said, that he had favoured them with his company. How did she know that it was the same bird? Oh, readily: the first time he came in he seemed quite at a loss where to settle down, flying hither and thither as if in search of a secure resting place; but when he came for the second season, he perched directly on that very bottle – and sang as if he was glad to be at home again.

We may pride ourselves today on our love of wild birds and yet the Victorians sometimes seem to put us to shame. Theirs, of course, was a more spacious and leisured age but, even so, this particular household really does seem to have leant over backwards to make its little feathered guest feel at home. I wonder whether A.F.T. was the master or the mistress of the house when he or she penned this letter to *Country Life* on 1 October 1898:

Our robin, beyond all others, exhibits a very strong individuality of his own . . . He has long been on visiting terms . . . He first introduced himself in July 1897 at the time when two small grandchildren were staying with us . . .

Having once gained a footing, Bobby proceeded to improve his acquaintance in the ordinary conventional way. At first he came into the drawing-room at the orthodox hour of afternoon tea. Here he was offered the usual fare of cake and bread and butter, but what he dearly loved was real rich Devonshire cream. It was most amusing to watch him flutter in delicious expectation over a plate of this tempting food spread on bread . . .

Becoming daily more familiar, he began to appear in the dining-room at meal times. And certainly never before was guest so warmly welcomed at all hours. The master of the house, forgetful of the dignity of weight of years, would even rise from his chair, open the window, and beg him to enter and make himself at home, which after a little coy dalliance at the sill, he generally did . . . A very charming addition did he make to the decorations of the table, especially on Christmas Day, when he was much in evidence . . .

He deeply resented any familiarity of touch, only now and then condescending to take bread and butter out of our hands if he was sufficiently hungry . . .

When spring drew near, we occasionally missed our little friend for a day or two, and sometimes discovered him flitting from tree to tree in musical converse with another of his species . . . At last, one day, we saw him fly out of the house with a bit of cotton wool in his beak. That settled the question, just as a man's friends know what to expect when they hear of his visiting house agents . . .

When summer came it brought a marked change in our little friend; for one thing, he never sang, and wore a preoccupied, anxious air. We decided family cares were weighing upon him; he grew much slimmer, though he came incessantly for food, and his appetite seemed voracious. After taking a few bites, he kept as large a piece as he could in his beak, flying round the room till he could get out with his booty. At last, one day, a singular spectacle presented itself. Coming into the drawing-room, we beheld Bobby on the piano, chirping encouragement to his frightened fledgling, who was flopping helplessly over the carpet. We ran for bread and butter, which Bobby took from our hands and put into his little one's mouth.

Cocking his head on one side, he looked at us with the self-congratulatory air of a proud parent, as if saying: 'This is my eldest son; what do you think of him?' He was certainly a sweet little creature, all fluffy brown, with light yellowish spots.

The Robin

On the following morning, no less than three fledglings appeared on the lawn, with another old bird, probably Mrs. Robin, though, with the modesty characteristic of her sex, she kept in the background.

On only two occasions has Bobby been known to spend the night indoors, and the first of these was so singular that it must be told. A little grand-daughter, aged six, had driven over with her father in the afternoon. As a heavy storm came on, it was arranged she should remain for the night, and a bed was prepared for her in a dressing-room adjoining that of her grandmother. Now Christine had never before slept in a room alone, and first was alarmed at the prospect, but on being promised a light burning, went to bed happy. What was our astonishment on going upstairs to find Bobby roosting on the lintel of her door, keeping guard. With daylight he was gone.

It is of course in the winter that the robin thrusts himself on our attention with his song; his red breast is then a tiny beacon in the snow:

> The redbreast smoulders in the waste of snow:
> His eye is large and bright, and to and fro
> He draws and draws his slender threads of sound
> Between the dark boughs and the freezing ground.
> *Anthony Rye: 'The Redbreast'*

That gentlest of eighteenth-century poets William Cowper caught perfectly the feeling of seeing a robin by chance when on a winter's walk:

> No noise is here, or none that hinders thought.
> The redbreast warbles still, but is content
> With slender notes, and more than half suppressed:
> Pleased with his solitude, and flitting light
> From spray to spray, where'er he rest he shakes
> From many a twig the pendent drops of ice,
> That twinkle in the withered leaves below.
> Stillness, accompanied with sounds so soft,
> Charms more than silence.
> *William Cowper (1731–1800): 'The Robin in Winter' (from 'The Task')*

Like most of us, W. H. Davies found the redbreast in winter impossible to resist:

Robin on a leafless bough,
Lord in Heaven, how he sings!
Now cold Winter's cruel Wind
Makes playmates of poor, dead things.

How he sings for joy this morn!
How his breast doth pant and glow!
Look you how he stands and sings,
Half-way up his legs in snow!

If these crumbs of bread were pearls,
And I had no bread at home,
He should have them for that song;
Pretty Robin Readbreast, Come.

W. H. Davies (1871–1940): from 'Robin Redbreast'

And Thomas Hardy magically makes us see the tiny hunched figure of a robin in the snow:

When winter frost
Makes earth as steel,
I search and search
But find no meal,
And most unhappy then I feel.

But when it lasts,
And snows still fall,
I get to feel
No grief at all,
For I turn to a cold stiff
Feathery ball!

Thomas Hardy (1840–1928): from 'The Robin'

In summer food is plentiful and he has other things to occupy him. To many he is then sadly missed.

Apart from the undoubted splendour of his red breast and all his winning ways, the robin, when all is said and done, is really rather a dumpy little bird. It took that acute observer John Ruskin, in a lecture at Oxford University in 1873, to sing the praises of his legs:

Hundreds of birds have longer and more imposing ones . . . but for real neatness, finish, and precision of action, commend me to his fine little ankles, and fine little feet; this long stilted process, as you know, corresponding to our ankle-bones. Commend me, I say, to the robin for use of his ankles – he is, of all birds, the pre-eminent and characteristic Hopper; none other so light, so pert, or so swift.

We must not, however, give too much credit to his legs in this matter. A robin's hop is a half flight; he hops, very essentially, with wings and tail, as well as with his feet, and the exquisitely rapid opening and quivering of the tail-feathers certainly give half the force to his leap. Leaps, I say; and you check at the word; and ought to check: you look at a bird hopping, and the motion is so much a matter of course to you, you never think how it is done. But do you think you would find it easy to hop like a robin if you had two – all but wooden – legs, like this?

There is one particular legend about the robin that may well have stemmed from his inquisitiveness in leading him to flit alongside travellers in the woods and forests. It was thought he would obligingly and charitably cover with moss and leaves any dead bodies he found. The wren assisted too. John Webster, Shakespeare's contemporary, wrote:

> Call for the robin redbreast and the wren,
> Since o'er shady groves they hover,
> And with leaves and flowers do cover
> The friendless bodies of unburied men.
>> *John Webster (c. 1580–c. 1625): 'The White Devil'*

And then, the babes in the wood:

> No burial these pretty babes
> Of any man receives
> Till Robin Redbreast piously
> Did cover them with leaves.

Robert Herrick, the seventeenth-century lyric poet, went so far as to hope that there would be a robin present to observe the last rites at his own burial:

> Laid out for dead, let thy last kindness be
> With leaves and moss-work for to cover me;
> And while the wood-nymphs my cold corpse inter,

Sing thou my dirge, sweet-warbling chorister!
For epitaph, in foliage, next write this:
Here, here the tomb of Robin Herrick is.

Robert Herrick (1591–1674)

My favourite lines for a dead robin came from the pen of Samuel Rogers, a man of letters born at Stoke Newington:

Tread lightly here, for here, 'tis said,
When piping winds are hushed around,
A small note wakes from underground,
Where now his tiny bones are laid.
No more in lone or leafless groves,
With ruffled wing and faded breast,
His friendless, homeless spirit roves;
Gone to the world where birds are blest!
Where never cat glides o'er the green,
Or school-boy's giant form is seen;
But love, and joy, and smiling Spring
Inspire their little souls to sing.

Samuel Rogers (1763–1855): 'Epitaph On a Robin Redbreast'
inscribed on an urn at Hafod, N. Wales

There are few sadder sights than a robin in mourning. It was on a glorious spring morning when walking my dog through a wooded part of Hampstead Heath that I spotted a most disconsolate hen robin sitting on a branch. Her bill was crammed with insects. Obviously, this was food intended for young. I suspect the fledglings had been taken by a jay. The little bird was a study in sorrow and allowed me so close that I could almost touch her. In her case, grief seemed too deep for song.

As a child, I well remember finding a dead robin in our garden in Surrey. There was still warmth in him and he looked perfect though the eyes were glazed. He may have had a heart attack or perhaps a cat had frightened him to death. My sister and I asked Mother for a cardboard shoe-box. We dug a little grave at the bottom of the garden and laid him gently in the box on a bed of leaves and grass. When we had covered it with earth, we fashioned a tiny cross from twigs to mark the place. I doubt if we would have done that for any bird other than a robin.

The Robin

George Darley, a nineteenth-century Irish poet would have understood:

> A little cross
> To tell my loss;
> A little bed
> To rest my head;
> A little tear is all I crave
> Upon my very little grave.
> I strew thy bed
> Who loved thy lays;
> The tear I shed,
> The cross I raise,
> With nothing more upon it than
> 'Here lies the little friend of man.'
>
> *George Darley (1795–1846)*

What do we know then of this 'little friend'? Even today most people are apt to think of a robin as being a male, a 'cock robin', probably because the sexes look exactly alike and both in winter have their own territories which they defend equally pugnaciously. It may well have been because of the hen robin's fighting qualities, that it was the popular idea long ago that 'cock robin's' mate was the more unassuming 'jenny wren' – William Blake was quite emphatic about it:

> The Robin and the Wren
> Are God Almighty's Cock and Hen,
> Him that harries their nest
> Never shall his soul have rest.
>
> *William Blake (1757–1827)*

The old nursery rhyme also insisted that there was some kind of liaison between them:

> Jenny Wren fell sick;
> Upon a merry time,
> In came Robin Redbreast,
> And brought her sops and wine.
>
> Eat well of the sop, Jenny,
> Drink well of the wine;

Thank you, Robin, kindly,
You shall be mine.

Jenny she got well,
And stood upon her feet,
And told Robin plainly
She loved him not a bit.

Robin, being angry,
Hopp'd on a twig,
Saying, Out upon you,
Fye upon you, bold-faced jig!

Anon.

The young robins, when they leave the nest, confuse a lot of people by their appearance because they lack the red breast. They are spotted and streaked with buff and brown and mottled on the breast. The all-important scarlet is not acquired until they have had their first moult in late summer.

The system of territories is a thoroughly sensible one because each bird or pair of birds become sole owners, as far as their own species are concerned, of an area of living-space that normally should provide a sufficiency of cover and food for them to survive and rear their young. The size of a territory will vary according to the number of birds in the area, but for a robin in town gardens it is usually about half an acre. To mark the boundaries of his domain the bird chooses a number of points from which to sing and thus proclaims his ownership. These 'song-posts' may be prominent and in the open or may equally well be positioned within the cover of a bush or tree. Some of the finest singing is heard when a male robin is trying to assert himself in the territory of another. In this case, the song is really a battle-cry.

If song doesn't do the trick, other methods of intimidation are tried. A robin will fly within a foot or two of his rival and flaunt his red breast in a threat display. This usually works so well that seldom is it necessary for battle to be joined.

So, although a robin may seem friendly to us, he is in fact a doughty fighter, especially in early spring, when he is full of aggression against any of his kind who may make so bold as to venture into his territory. It is clear that in repelling invaders the colour red is crucial. David Lack in his *Life of the Robin* tells of a series of experiments carried out by placing a stuffed robin close to a wild one. In most cases the specimen was attacked fiercely, but only so long as it contained red feathers. When similar experiments were tried in which the red breast was painted brown it was no longer attacked.

When it comes to courtship the robin is no great gallant. In mid-winter the cock bird will simply sing to advertise his presence, but it is the female who does the mate-hunting and the choosing. Unobtrusively she slips into the undergrowth nearby and, if the cock tolerates her presence for a week or two, gradually she latches on to him and a pair is formed.

Unlike most birds, robins do not indulge in display ceremonies, but a bond is formed between them with the feeding of the hen by the cock. This is a sure way to distinguish the sexes. The hen behaves exactly like a young robin being fed by a parent: lowering her wings and vibrating with excitement. It is well worth the trouble of rising early on a morning in late March, when you might see for yourself, as a privileged spectator, this charming little feeding ceremony. The cock also feeds the hen during incubation so that she is able to spend more time sitting on the eggs. Food mainly consists of insects or spiders, centipedes and so on, but seeds, fruit and berries are also eaten. In hard weather robins are also attracted by bread, seed or fat.

The nest itself is built by the hen alone, as is the case with most of our songbirds, although the male will sometimes bring nesting material. It is made of moss, dead leaves and grass and the lining is of hair or wool with perhaps a few feathers. It might be placed almost anywhere but is usually only a few feet above the ground. I have found several in grassy banks; other favourite places are a hole in a tree or a crevice in an ivy-clad wall. The robin is often eccentric in its choice of a nesting site. A gentleman named Allen H. P. Stoneham wrote to *Country Life* on 15 September 1900:

I have seen illustrations in your paper of curious places selected by birds for building their nests, but I think that the case I am about to relate is as curious and as bold as any. This robin's nest was built in some clogs hanging on my stable-yard wall; these clogs were in constant use except for three days, from a Friday to the following Monday morning. On the Monday, one of the grooms on taking down the clogs to wash the dog-cart found a robin's nest in one. He hung the clogs up again and told me. I watched the clogs daily. Four eggs were laid and four robins hatched out, and notwithstanding that horses and carriages are constantly in and out of the yard and that the clogs hung close to the gate where the grooms were passing all day long.

Then Edward Jesse, a well-known naturalist who lived from 1780 to 1868, wrote this account in *Gleanings in Natural History*:

A gentleman in my neighbourhood had directed one of his waggons to be packed with sundry hampers and boxes, intending to send it to Worthing, where he was going himself. For some reason, his going was delayed; and he therefore directed that the waggon should be placed in a shed in his yard, packed as it was, till it should be convenient for him to send it off. While it was in the shed, a pair of robins built their nest among some straw in the waggon, and had hatched their young just before it was sent away. One of the old birds, instead of being frightened away by the motion of the waggon, only left its nest from time to time for the purpose of flying to the nearest hedge for food for its young; and thus, alternately affording warmth and nourishment to them, it arrived at Worthing. The affection of this bird having been observed by the waggoner, he took care in un-loading, not to disturb the robin's nest, and my readers will, I am sure, be glad to hear that the robin and its young ones returned in safety to Walton Heath, being the place from which it had set out. Whether it was the male or female robin which kept with the waggon, I have not been able to ascertain; but most probably the latter, as what will not a mother's love and a mother's tenderness induce her to perform? The distance the waggon went in going and returning could not have been less than one hundred miles.

More recently there have been reports of a robin nesting in the bonnet of a car, on the seat of a farm tractor and even in an aircraft engine. The favouring of discarded kettles, saucepans or watering cans is quite commonplace, but David Lack surely came across the swiftest happening when he wrote: 'The record for speed goes to a Basingstoke pair. A gardener hung up his coat in the tool-shed at 9.15 a.m., and when he took it down to go off to lunch at 1 p.m. there was an almost complete robin's nest in one of the pockets.'

26

Recalling Wordsworth's description of the robin as 'The pious bird with the scarlet breast', it is no surprise that places of worship are also chosen. In F. A. Morris's *A History of British Birds* we read:

A few years ago, a pair of robins took up their abode in the Parish Church of Hampton, Warwickshire, and affixed their nest to the Church Bible, as it lay on the reading-desk. The vicar would not allow the birds to be disturbed and therefore supplied himself with another Bible, from which he read the Lessons of the Service.

[And again:] A similar instance occurred at Collingbourne Kingston Church, in Wiltshire, on the 13th of April 1834; the Clerk on looking out for the lessons of the day, perceived something under the Bible in the reading-desk, and in a hollow place, occasioned by the Bible's resting on a raised ledge, found a Robin's nest, containing two eggs. The bird not having been disturbed laid four more which were hatched on the 4th of May. The still more extraordinary part of the story is that the cock bird actually brought food in its bill during Divine Service, which is performed twice every Sunday; and it is further highly creditable to the parishioners, particularly the junior part of them, that the birds were never molested, and not an attempt was even suspected to be made on the nest and eggs deposited in so hallowed a spot.

The usual number of eggs laid is five; they are white with reddish brown spots. Incubation lasts thirteen to fourteen days. After another fourteen days, the young leave the nest and three weeks later they are independent. There are two and sometimes three broods. Most males are residents, whereas only about a third of the females remain for the winter. The rest migrate locally or to southern Europe. As already observed, the hen robins which stay behind behave like males and find their own territories, singing and fighting to maintain them until early spring, when the mating procedure begins all over again.

The robin's song is not particularly distinguished – a silvery thread of sound – but he sings, with varying degrees of vigour, nearly all the year round. It is in winter, when most other birds are silent, that his little song becomes a great joy.

Confiding and trusting as the robin is, his friendship, at least until the Protection of Birds Acts were passed, was often abused. His very trustingness made him easy to trap, and at one time many of his kind ended up in cages. Yet, even in the bad old days, fewer robins were subjected to captivity than most other songbirds. People felt that somehow it wasn't right.

In the early years of the last century, Mayhew in *London Labour and the London Poor* wrote:

Redbreasts are a portion of the street-sold birds, but the catch is not large, not exceeding 3,000 with a mortality of about a third, Even this number, small as it is when compared with the numbers of other singing birds sold, is got rid of with difficulty. There is a popular feeling repugnant to the imprisonment, or coercion in any way, of a robin, and this no doubt has its influence in moderating the demand. The redbreast is sold, when young, both in the shops and streets, for 1s., when caged and singing, sometimes for £1. These birds are considered to sing best by candlelight.

As William Blake so rightly observed:

A Robin Redbreast in a Cage
Puts all Heaven in a Rage,

But not only were songbirds put in cages. An interesting side-light on just how much our attitude to wild birds has changed comes from this letter to *The Times* of 8 March 1869. It was signed, simply, Indignant, Lincoln's Inn:

Sir, This (Sunday) morning, the 7th March, I counted from a railway carriage thirteen shooting parties along one side of the Great Eastern Railway between Stratford and Tottenham stations alone. One shot was fired from the railway at a robin perched upon the telegraph wire – a fine sitting shot! Surely, sir, it is time to put a tax upon guns!

It was not all persecution. Birds have always had their protectors, but seldom such gifted versifiers as Thomas, Lord Erskine who was living on the north London heights of Hampstead at the end of the eighteenth century. He wrote this felicitous sonnet, as he put it: 'On letting out into my garden at Hampstead seven robins, which I bought in a cage of a boy, who had just caught them by means of a decoy bird, in a field near my house.'

The Robin

The Liberated Robins

Now harmless songsters, ye are free!
Yet stay awhile and sing to me;
And make these sheltered bounds your home,
Nor towards those dangerous meadows roam.
Your ruddy bosoms pant with fear
But no dark snare awaits you here.
No artful note of tame decoy
Shall lure you from your native joy.
These blossom shrubs are all your own,
And lawns with sweetest berries strewn;
And when bleak winter thins your store,
This friendly hand shall furnish more;
Nor shall my window shutters fold
Against my robins numb with cold.

Thomas, Lord Erskine, September 2nd, 1798

The robins' thank you was penned for them by no less a person than the noble Lord's daughter, the Hon. Mrs Holland:

The Robins' Reply to their Benefactor

We happy robins, here set free,
With grateful hearts will sing to thee;
Henceforward this shall be our home,
We promise never far to roam,
But rest, devoid of every fear,
Since no dark snare awaits us here.
Nor hazard these our peaceful joys
By answering to tame decoys.
We'll eat thy berries thickly sown,
And look upon them as our own.
We thank thee for our promised store –
What can poor robins give thee more?
To us thou art already blest,
And great's the joy within thy breast!
And oh! may thou who set us free
Enjoy in peace sweet liberty.
We'll sing to thee all day, till death
Deprives us of our little breath.

And then our sons shall sing to thee,
For thou hast given them liberty.
If they, like us, shall be trepanned,
Once more stretch out thy friendly hand,
And snatch them from their hapless fate –
Restore them to their native state,
And feed and shelter them from ill,
And be their guardian angel still.

And this may well be the song of blessing those grateful robins have been singing ever since to all their benefactors everywhere:

God bless the field and bless the furrow
Stream and branch and rabbit burrow
Hill and stone and flower and tree
From Bristol Town to Weatherby
Bless the sun and bless the sleet
Bless the lane and bless the street
Bless the night and bless the day
From Somerset and all the way
To the meadows of Cathay.

Bless the minnow, bless the whale
Bless the rainbow and the hail
Bless the nest and bless the leaf
Bless the righteous and the thief
Bless the wind and bless the fin
Bless the air I travel in
Bless the mill and bless the mouse
Bless the miller's bricken house
Bless the earth and bless the sea
God bless you and God bless me.

Traditional

2

The Blue Tit

Lithest, gaudiest harlequin!
Prettiest tumbler ever seen,
Light of heart and light of limb,
What is now become of him?

A question put by William Wordsworth who would probably have
agreed that if the redbreast is Britain's top bird, then the blue tit or
tom tit must come a very close second.

In autumn and winter no bird is a more welcome guest at countless bird-tables and seen to best advantage when exercising his considerable acrobatic skills, to get at the seeds, nuts or fat in hanging
food-containers. I sometimes get letters asking me where the blue
tits vanish to in summertime when clearly the charm of their antics
at the feeders is sadly missed. The answer of course is that they
usually return to their breeding territories in neighbouring woodland where oak trees in most years provide a plentiful supply of
caterpillars.

In our Hampstead cottage my wife Nan and I are regularly
favoured by winter visits from a merry host of blue, great and coal
tits. There is no problem in identification. The cobalt-blue crown is
most distinctive, while the great tit is not only larger but has a
broad black band down the centre of its yellow breast. The coal tit
is the smallest of the three and has a white patch on the back of its
glossy black head. Although only four-and-a-half miles from the
centre of London, the eight hundred or more acres of Hampstead
Heath, containing large areas of oak, beech and birch, provide
abundant food for the tit family in summer. I don't know of any
comparable open space within the limits of any other great city in

the world. To call it a heath is really a misnomer as there is such a variety of scene: there are hints of the downs by the sea, of moorland, marsh and woodland – all in exquisite union.

That great naturalist W. H. Hudson also knew the Heath and was especially fascinated by the last remnant of the old Middlesex forest, now known as Kenwood. Writing at the turn of the century, he told of a keeper's wife who one night saw what she took to be some kind of dog trotting across the lawn; she called to it but receiving no response, ran after it into the wood to discover that she had in fact been chasing a large badger.

Sadly, the badgers are now no more, but there are plenty of rabbits and I have twice seen a handsome dog fox as bold as brass in daylight. Hudson also counted forty-three species of bird breeding on the Heath and that number is happily about the same today. In all, ninety-one different kinds were recorded in 1977 including such shy birds as water rails and snipe.

So when in 1974 I was invited to cover wildlife stories for the BBC 'Nationwide' programme I suggested they might do worse for a start than look at the birds in my small walled garden in Hampstead. The idea was to show some of the fascinating birdlife that can be seen close to the centre of a big city.

As it was January, I knew there would be plenty of birds to see. Every winter for years Nan and I have regularly filled containers of nuts and fat and hung them from the slender branches of a wild cherry tree that arches over the path leading to the front door. Our dining room is very small but the window looks straight out on to this tree containing the Dougall snack-bar. The producer, cameraman and sound-recordist crammed into the little room with their equipment.

It was a day of hard frost and in the garden there was plenty of action. This was mainly supplied by the regulars – the blue, coal and great tits which were seen to best possible advantage. They were also joined from time to time by that handsome, torpedo-shaped little bird, the nuthatch with its grey upper-parts, buff underneath, white throat and distinctive black eye stripe.

There was another bird I very much hoped would drop in on that day of all days. For some weeks a great spotted woodpecker had been in the habit of swooping down about lunchtime. By a quarter past one the bird still hadn't shown up, but the cameraman said he would stay at the ready by the window just in case. When the rest of us returned from a visit to an adjoining pub, we found him quite jubilant.

He said the woodpecker had swept in dramatically, like a demon king, with the small birds scattering in all directions. I knew the vivid scarlet, black and white plumage would look most impressive in close-up and so it proved. In fact, when the sceptical 'Nationwide' editor at the BBC Lime Grove studios saw the rushes of the film, he thought we had cheated by including some material from the archives. He needed some convincing that every foot of film had been shot that morning in my Hampstead garden. Anyway, it made a colourful contribution to the day's programme and opened a lot of eyes to the variety and fascination of birdlife to be seen near the centre of London and other big cities.

Of all the titmouse family, the blue tit is the general favourite because of its eye-catching colour. It is curious that such a sprightly, vivacious, diminutive bird should ever have been known as the nun, but its blue cap and white cheeks must have earned it the name. In 1789 the great Gilbert White wrote this description to a fellow naturalist Thomas Pennant Esq.:

The blue titmouse, or nun, is a great frequenter of houses, and a general devourer. Beside insects, it is very fond of flesh; for it frequently picks bones on dunghills: it is a vast admirer of suet, and haunts butchers' shops. When a boy, I have known twenty on a morning caught with snap mouse-traps, baited with tallow or suet.

Mercifully we have come a long way since the eighteenth century. He continues:

It will also pick holes in apples left on the ground, and be well entertained with the seeds on the head of a sun-flower. The blue, marsh, and great titmice will, in very severe weather, carry away barley and oat straws from the sides of ricks.

Presumably they did this in a frantic search for insects, but the hay-ricks have vanished and so now suburban gardens have become an important source of food. Walter de la Mare wrote these lines after watching a titmouse taking his fill from a dangling coconut:

Titmouse

If you would happy company win,
Dangle a palm-nut from a tree,
Idly in green to sway and spin,
Its snow-pulped kernel for bait; and see
　　A nimble titmouse enter in.

Out of earth's vast unknown of air,
Out of all summer, from wave to wave,
He'll perch, and prank his feathers fair,
Jangle a glass-clear wildering stave,
　　And take his commons there –

This tiny son of life; this spright
By momentary Human sought,
Plume will his wing in the dappling light,
Clash timbrel shrill and gay –
And into Time's enormous Nought,
　　Sweet-fed will flit away.

Ornithologists are apt to think now that coconut is an indigestible food for the tits, and harmful to the young, but there is no doubt of the birds' liking for it. Certainly, dried coconut should never be given to them as that can cause serious harm. In general it is inadvisable to put out food for the birds in spring or summer when there are young in the nest. Insects or other natural food provided by the parents is by far the best.

It is curious to think nowadays that a talk by an ornithologist over the wireless once gave the august Director-General of the BBC a headache. The expert was listing the food different birds like to eat. A good lady, somewhere in the Shires, was entering her drawing room from the garden. As she stepped in, these fateful three words 'tits like coconuts' emanated from the loudspeaker. That was enough for her! She rushed to the set, switched it off and sat down to write Sir John Reith a snorter. She accused him of polluting the ether with foul language, debasing womanhood and heaven knows what else. Reith's reply was short and to the point: 'Dear Madam, if you had only continued listening you would also have heard that robins like worms.'

Apart from the pleasure and amusement derived from watching the acrobatic antics of blue tits at food-containers, you may be privileged to see some of their courtship behaviour in early spring. I was puzzled for some time by a pair of birds in my Suffolk garden.

Towards evening they appeared to carry out a little ceremony near an old apple tree. Long after most birds had gone to roost, these two would chase each other round the garden in a high state of excitement making short swooping flights. It hadn't occurred to me that this was part of the courtship procedure until I came across a passage in a book written by E. A. Armstrong in 1944 entitled *The Way Birds Live*. He wrote:

The hen blue tit nearly always goes to roost earlier than her mate. But before retiring to bed they have a little frolic together. If she is already in her roosting-hole when the male arrives, he calls her out in order that they may have their game, which consists mainly of a good-natured chase.

It seems that at least some blue tits remain paired through the winter.

There is very little difference in the appearance of the sexes. The female is a trifle smaller and her colours are not so bright; the blue stripe on the breast is shorter and not so well defined. In addition to the bedtime ceremony, the male in spring puts on a flight display: gliding down to the nest-hole with wings spread like a butterfly. The female takes charge of the nest-building but solicits food from the male with a wing-shivering display, which usually results in the offering of a green caterpillar. As she will have to produce more than her own weight in eggs, she obviously needs all the food she can get.

Blue tits rival robins in the oddity of the places in which they choose to nest. When garden pumps were in general use in the last century, even these were favoured, although the bird would be continually disturbed and the nest often partly destroyed by the action of the handle. In Morris's *A History of British Birds* Bishop Stanley is quoted as saying:

It happened that during the time of building and laying the eggs, the pump had not been in use; and when again set going, the female was sitting, and it was naturally supposed that the motion of the pump handle would drive her away. The young brood, however, were hatched safely, without any other misfortune than the loss of a part of the tail of the sitting bird, which was rubbed off by the friction of the pump handle.

Morris then recounts this grisly occurrence:

The most extraordinary situation, however, that I have heard or read of for the location of the nest of this, or of any other species of bird, was within the jaws of the skeleton of a man who had been executed and hung in chains for murder.

After that, it is quite a relief to read of this gentler happening near Eastleigh in Hampshire. *Country Life* for 2 September 1899 tells us:

A lady has taken advantage of the liking that tom tits have for building in letter-boxes. She has had two sham letter-boxes made with lids which lift up. In each of these a tom tit has built this year, and, while the birds were sitting, anyone could go and lift up the lids of the boxes and look at them. They never moved, and the whole arrangement made a very pretty and interesting side-show in the garden.

I only hope the birds survived all the attention.

At our Suffolk cottage for some years now blue tits have reared young in a nest-box I fixed near the entrance to a woodshed. It is always advisable to site the box so that it will not be in the full glare of the sun nor in a place where rain might penetrate. Most important of all – never site a nest-box where a cat might be able to reach into it.

Len Howard in her marvellous book *Birds as Individuals,* in which she wrote of the birds she lived with at her cottage in Sussex, told of an unhappy experience with a cat:

It was a spring morning, three months after my little cottage had been built, and I was busy within, near an open door, when a Blue Tit came fluttering up with cries of distress. She hovered agitatedly close in front of me, her eyes fixed on mine, crying as I had never heard a Blue Tit cry before; it was at once obvious something was wrong and she was asking for my help. Her mate was with her but perched just outside, watching me intently. Directly I went out she stopped crying and they led me to her nesting-box, flying on in front and at suitable perches on the way, turning round to see that I followed. The whole of her nest had been pulled in fragments from the nesting-box and her twelve eggs lay scattered over the hard wooden floor of the box. The lid was shut, so it appeared a cat had clawed out the nest in pieces through the entrance hole.

The lesson here is that nest-boxes should be deeper than five inches and for blue tits the entrance hole should be just an inch, or to be precise one and one-eighth of an inch, across. Any larger and a sparrow or starling may well intrude. It is always best to obtain a box from one of the recognised bird societies. Many of the boxes I have seen for sale are also much too cramped inside and a bird will only use them if there is nothing else available.

The clutch of eggs has been known to number as many as nineteen in a woodland site, although eleven or twelve is more usual. In gardens the clutch is usually smaller – about seven or eight, because the parent birds have greater difficulty in feeding their young. The supply of caterpillars is often sparse and beakfuls of greenfly from the roses are a poor substitute. Somehow, blue tits are able, in a quite remarkable way, to adjust the size of their clutches to suit the local conditions. In woodland, probably not more than ten per cent of the eggs laid will eventually become breeding birds; the garden birds are lucky to raise half their broods and many of the young when they leave the nest are in a rather weak state.

Morris's *A History of British Birds* quotes this account from the *Journal of a Naturalist*:

I was lately exceedingly pleased in witnessing the maternal care and intelligence of this bird; for the poor thing had its young ones in the hole of a wall, and the nest had been nearly all drawn out of the crevice by the paw of a cat, and part of its brood devoured. In revisiting its family, the bird discovered a portion of it remaining, though wrapped up and hidden in the tangled moss and feathers of their bed, and it then drew the whole of the nest back into the place from whence it had been taken, unrolled and re-settled the remaining little ones, fed them with the usual attentions, and finally succeeded in rearing them. The parents of even this reduced family laboured with great perseverance to supply its wants, one or other of them bringing a grub, caterpillar, or some insect, at intervals of less than a minute through the day, and probably in the earlier part of the morning more frequently; but if we allow that they brought food to the hole every minute for fourteen hours, and provided for their own wants also, it will admit of perhaps a thousand grubs a day, for the requirements of one, and that a diminished brood, and gives us some comprehension of the infinite number requisite for the summer nutriment of our soft-billed birds, and the great distances gone over by such as have young ones, in their numerous trips from hedge to tree in the hours specified, when they have full broods to support.

It has been calculated that a total of about ten thousand trips is the average to rear a whole brood.

After nineteen days the fledglings leave the nest following their parents from tree to tree. It takes at least another fortnight before they can feed themselves and this is their period of greatest danger. Provided they survive, young tits of all species then form flocks while the adults are accomplishing their moult.

At least the young blue tit has agility, boldness and intelligence to help him survive. He is a bonnie fighter and seems to know no fear. He will even take on a kestrel and is in the forefront when it comes to mobbing an owl. As for applied intelligence, we all know what happens to the milk bottles on the doorstep. At our cottage the situation is made even worse by Tess, the family pointer. She is no slouch herself and, once the tits have removed the caps and had a few sips of the cream, she has discovered the delights of insinuating her long pink tongue into the neck of the bottles like a green woodpecker in search of ants. I can't think why we haven't all long ago succumbed to foot and mouth disease.

Blue tits have also sailed through experimental intelligence tests requiring them to remove a sequence of pegs to get at food or open matchboxes with food concealed inside. Some of their behaviour is very puzzling. Blue tits in the autumn will occasionally attack a wall, tearing away at putty or a piece of plaster. At least the putty has some food value – it contains fish oil. Again, if they get inside a house they might well attack the wallpaper. This is probably because, being woodland birds, they are accustomed to ripping the bark off trees in a search for insects. But nobody really knows.

Few in our time have understood the intelligence of birds better than that remarkable lady Len Howard. In her book *Birds as Individuals* she wrote:

One December day a blue tit, new to my cottage, flew into the room through the small fanlight which in winter is usually the only open window. It tried to get out again by a closed one on the opposite side of the room, fluttering and banging itself against the pane in panic-stricken efforts. Another blue tit, familiar with my room and the fanlight, saw from outside the closed window this frightened tit struggling against the panes. After watching a moment with a worried expression, the outside tit flew hurriedly round to the other side of the cottage, entered through the fanlight, paused a second on the sill to call gently, but finding no notice was taken the rescuer flew across the room and touched the fluttering tit, who immediately turned round to follow the rescuer back across the room and out of the narrowly-opened fanlight. In going to fetch the stranger-tit the rescuer showed thought amounting to reasoning power.

Of course all this is highly arguable but I for one am more than content to defer to the admirable Miss Howard.

And a last tribute from Walter de la Mare:

The Tomtit

Twilight had fallen, austere and grey,
The ashes of a wasted day,
When, tapping at the window-pane,
My visitor had come again,
To peck late supper at his ease –
A morsel of suspended cheese.

What ancient code, what Morse knew he –
This eager little mystery –
That, as I watched, from lamp-lit room,
Called on some inmate of my heart to come
Out of its shadows – filled me then
With love, delight, grief, pining, pain,
Scarce less than had he angel been?

Suppose, such countenance as that,
Inhuman, deathless, delicate,
Had gazed this winter moment in –
Eyes of an ardour and beauty no
Star, no Sirius could show!

Well, it were best for such as I
To shun direct divinity;
Yet not stay heedless when I heard
The tip-tap nothings of a tiny bird.

3

The Cuckoo

The cuckoo's a bonny bird,
He sings as he flies;
He brings us good tidings;
He tells us no lies.

He drinks the cold water
To keep his voice clear;
And he'll come again
In the spring of the year.

Anon.

For most country folk and for many town-dwellers too spring is not felt to have truly arrived until the cuckoo is heard. Last April, it was on the 25th, when I awoke to hear those two marvellous, joyous, hollow-sounding notes. My watch said it was 5.30 a.m. Outside, there was no more than a glimmer of grey; Hampstead was still asleep. So was my wife. For some reason she didn't feel disposed to share my enthusiasm. If we had been in the country, I don't suppose I would have roused her, but, situated only four-and-a-half miles from the centre of London, the sound to me was all the more magical and exciting. The bird continued calling for about twenty minutes but he can only have been passing through because, sadly, I didn't hear him again.

His two notes seemed to hold all the fleeting nature of spring:

I waited, listened; came again
Across the distance of the rain
'Cuckoo' so faint and far away

41

It sounded out of yesterday,
Making me start with sudden fear
Lest spring that had seemed new and near
Was gone already. A sparrow hopped
In white plum-tree and blossom dropped.
Andrew Young (1885–1971): extract from 'The Cuckoo'

Once, in the country, it was thought to be a misfortune to hear the cuckoo for the first time from one's bed:

There was a superstition that where or in whatever condition you happened to be when you heard the cuckoo the first time in the Spring, so you would remain for the next twelvemonth; for which reason it was a misfortune to hear her first in bed, since it might mean a long illness. This, by-the-way, may have been a pleasant fable invented to get milkmaids up early of a morning.
Richard Jefferies (1848–1887): 'The Gamekeeper at Home'

There is also a country legend about the cuckoo's loneliness. This is to the effect that once at a Holy Festival of the Virgin all the birds ceased work to worship her, but the cuckoo alone carried on working at his nest. Since then he has never been allowed to build another and wanders the earth alone, parted forever from domestic joys.

Many of us have strangely mixed feelings about the cuckoo. Edward Thomas, the nature writer and poet, who was cut down by shell-blast at Arras one spring day in 1917, put these thoughts into marvellous words:

The first snowdrop, the first blackbird's song or peewit's love cry, the first hawthorn leaves, are as nothing even to those who regard them, compared with the cuckoo's note, while there are many for whom it is the one powerfully significant natural thing throughout the year, apart from broad gradual changes, such as the greening or the baring of the woods. The old become fearful lest they should not hear it: having heard it, they fear lest it should be for the last time. It has been accepted as the object upon which we concentrate whatever feeling we have towards the beginning of spring. It constitutes a natural, unmistakable festival. We wish to hear it, we are eager and anxious about it, we pause when it reaches us, as if perhaps it might be bringing more than it ever brought yet. Vaguely enough, as a rule, we set much store by this first hearing, and the expectancy does not fail to bring its reward of at least a full and intense impression. And for this purpose the cuckoo's note is perfectly suited. It is loud, clear, brief, and distinct, never in danger of being lost in a chorus of its own or another kind: it has a human and also a ghostly quality which earns it the reputation of sadness or joyousness at different times.

Edward Thomas (1879–1917): extract from 'The Last Sheaf'

Michael Bruce, a young eighteenth-century poet, who died when he was twenty-one, gave the cuckoo an unqualified welcome:

Hail, beauteous stranger of the grove!
Thou messenger of Spring!
Now Heaven repairs thy rural seat,
And woods thy welcome sing.

What time the daisy decks the green,
Thy certain voice we hear;
Hast thou a star to guide thy path,
Or mark the rolling year?

Delightful visitant! with thee
I hail the time of flowers,
And hear the sound of music sweet
From birds among the bowers.

The schoolboy, wandering through the wood
To pull the primrose gay,
Starts, the new voice of spring to hear,
And imitates thy lay.

What time the pea puts on the bloom,
Thou fliest thy vocal vale,
An annual guest in other lands,
Another spring to hail.

Sweet bird! thy bower is ever green,
Thy sky is ever clear;
Thou hast no sorrow in thy song,
No winter in thy year.

A Celebration of Birds

O could I fly, I'd fly with thee!
We'd make with joyful wing,
Our annual visit o'er the globe,
Companions of the spring.

Michael Bruce (1746–1767): 'Ode to the Cuckoo'

Like young Michael Bruce, Wordsworth had no doubts at all: the cuckoo was a mysterious, blessed bird and to hear it in spring was to rejoice:

O blithe Newcomer! I have heard,
I hear thee and rejoice.
O Cuckoo! shall I call thee Bird,
Or but a wandering Voice!

While I am lying on the grass
Thy twofold shout I hear,
From hill to hill it seems to pass,
At once far off, and near.

Though babbling only to the Vale,
Of sunshine and of flowers,
Thou bringest unto me a tale
Of visionary hours.

Thrice welcome, darling of the Spring!
Even yet thou art to me
No bird, but an invisible thing,
A voice, a mystery;

The same whom in my school-boy days
I listened to; that Cry
Which made me look a thousand ways
In bush, and tree, and sky.

To seek thee did I often rove
Through woods and on the green;
And thou wert still a hope, a love;
Still longed for, never seen.

And I can listen to thee yet;
Can lie upon the plain

And listen, till I do beget
That golden time again.

O blessed Bird! The earth we pace
Again appears to be
An unsubstantial, faery place;
That is fit home for Thee!

That great Puritan John Bunyan, on the other hand, was not among the cuckoo's admirers. He expressed himself most forcibly:

Thy notes do not first welcome in our Spring
Nor dost thou its first token to us bring,
Birds less than thou by far, like prophets do
Tell us 'tis coming, tho' not by cuckoo.
Nor dost thou summer have away with thee,
Though thou a yawling, bawling cuckoo be!

About this time, somewhere around the middle of the seventeenth century, Bunyan tells us: 'I was never out of the Bible either by reading or meditation.' Is it possible that his views on the bird might have been coloured by the good book?

Moses in Leviticus 11:16 and again in Deuteronomy 14:15 warns the children of Israel to hold the 'cuckow' in abomination. The bird is listed mistakenly with scavengers and mentioned in the company of hawks. This may have given rise to a belief at one time among Bible-reading country folk that, come the winter, the cuckoo changes into a hawk. Even today, a cuckoo in flight is often mistaken for a male sparrow-hawk. Both are predominantly grey, but the cuckoo has pointed wings and longer tail feathers which are spotted and tipped with white. At rest, the cuckoo's bill is seen to be much more slender and less sharply curved.

Until the last century there was only the haziest understanding of migration, and country legends maintained that the cuckoo hibernated in mud or spent the winter curled up in a hollow branch. Let us hearken unto Francis Willoughby Esquire of Middleton in the County of Warwick, Fellow of the Royal Society, and a prominent Ornithologist. He expounded these ideas in 1628. The spelling and use of capitals are Mr Willoughby's own:

The Cuckoo

What becomes of the Cuckoo in the Winter-time, whether hiding her self in hollow Trees, or other holes and Caverns, she lies torpid, and at the return of the Spring revives again; or rather at the approach of Winter, being impatient of cold, shifts place and departs into hot Countrys, is not as yet to me certainly known.

Later in his treatise he cites the testimony of one Theophilus Molitor, as a credible person and eyewitness of this lurking of Cuckows in hollow trees:

His Grandfathers Servants, having stocked up in a certain meadow some old dry, rotten willows, and brought them home, and cast the heads of two of them into the Furnace to heat the Stove, heard as they were in the Stove a Cuckow singing three times. Wondring at this cry of the Cuckow in the Winter-time, out they go, and drawing the heads of the Willows out of the Furnace, in the one of them they observed something move; wherefore taking an Axe they opened the hole, and thrusting in their hands, first they plucked out nothing but meer feathers. Afterwards they got hold of a living Animal, that was the very Cuckow, and drew it out. It was indeed brisk and lively, but wholly naked and bare of feathers, and without any Winter-provision of food, which Cuckow the Boys kept two whole years in the Stove.

At the end of that time the luckless 'Cuckow' no doubt saw the error of its ways.

In 'Norton Wood', T. E. Brown the nineteenth-century Manx-man poet expresses exuberantly the thrill of hearing the first cuckoo:

> And, coming home,
> Well laden, as we clomb
> Sweet Walton hill,
> A cuckoo shouted with a will –
> 'Cuckoo! cuckoo!' the first we've heard!
> 'Cuckoo! cuckoo!' God bless the bird!
> Scarce time to take his breath,
> And now 'Cuckoo!' he saith –
> 'Cuckoo! cuckoo!' three cheers!
> And let the welkin ring!
> He has not folded wing
> Since he last saw Algiers.

T. E. Brown: extract from 'Norton Wood'

Normally the bird arrives in this country from its winter quarters in Africa about the second or third week of April. The annual letters to *The Times* reflect the national concern. The call of the cuckoo is not the most difficult sound in nature to reproduce and, while genuine March arrivals are not unknown, they should be treated with reserve. As for a February arrival that calls for a hefty grain of salt. And yet in 1898 a reader of *Country Life* claimed to have heard the bird on 14 February, St Valentine's Day, in Richmond Park. This prompted a letter, dated 18 March 1898, from a gentleman who signed himself 'Cuculus':

Sir, The cuckoo referred to in one of your recent notes as heard on St. Valentine's Day in Richmond Park is certainly a bird to be received *cum grano salis*; which grain should be put on his tail, that he may, if possible, be identified. But the story, whether the cuckoo be a true bird or an unfeathered biped, has called to my mind a common belief of the rustic people in this part of the country – East Sussex – that the cuckoo is a bird that is kept in a cage all winter and only let out in spring, by an old woman living in Ashdown Forest.

No one, curiously, seems to know the name of this old woman, nor where she lives. It is to be supposed that there are more than one of these old women living in different parts of the country with a similar penchant for cuckoos, otherwise it seems hard to understand how the land is peopled with its cuckoos. But when you put this kind of question, bordering on criticism, to the folk of East Sussex, they relapse into their invincible stolidity and no more is to be got out of them. Possibly one of these old women – can a cuckoo clock in the possession of some reputed witch be the origin of the story? – may have let one of her pets go about on St. Valentine's Day in the neighbourhood of Richmond. But it is earlier in the year than she can generally bring herself to part with it.

The males are the first to arrive and select a feeding area, calling incessantly by day and sometimes by night as well. The females on arrival are silent until ready to mate, when their strange 'water-bubbling' cry is heard. This is nothing like as familiar as the call of the male and there are many country people who do not even know the sound.

The former Statesman and observer of nature, Lord Grey of Fallodon, was lucky enough to see the mating and wrote this short account in his book *The Charm of Birds* which first appeared in 1927:

The Cuckoo

I was sitting under a lime tree at the Hampshire cottage; the spreading branches concealed me from outside view, but looking out from beneath them much could be seen. A cuckoo came flying and lit on the branch of a poplar only a few yards in front. Having chosen its perch, the bird uttered the loud 'water-bubbling' notes. A male cuckoo was immediately heard at some distance; it came, cuckooing vehemently as it flew, and lit on the branch by the side of the first bird. There what Chaucer calls 'a spring observance' took place. In this instance there was no sign of a second male in the neighbourhood; there was nothing, therefore, to suggest that the two cuckoos were not paired like monogamous birds. Sometimes, however, the 'water-bubbling' note provokes the cuckooing and pursuit of more than one male bird. The familiar 'cuckoo' is thus, on some occasions, an answer to the call of the female; but generally, like other birds' song, it is an expression of sheer joy, vigour, challenge or excitement.

Until patient research and photography recorded the event, it was thought that the female cuckoo laid its egg on the ground close by the chosen nest. The theory was that it then picked up its egg and placed it in the nest after removing one of the eggs already there.

Now, we know better. In 1973 a remarkable study of the whole process was begun in Cambridgeshire by the ornithologist and photographer Ian Wyllie. He helped obtain the unforgettable egg-laying sequence used in the BBC film *The Private Life of the Cuckoo*. Among other things this showed that eleven seconds is all the time it takes for the parasite cuckoo, after arrival at a nest, to lay her own egg and then make off with one of the host bird's eggs in her bill. This she either eats or drops. A couple of days later, she will lay again in another nest and so continue at intervals until she has up to twelve or thirteen eggs deposited like tiny time-bombs in the nests of other unsuspecting birds in her territory.

Maurice Tibbles who made the film with Ian Wyllie wrote a memorable account for *Country Life* of 17 April 1975. In this case, the nest being invaded was that of a reed warbler. The film camera was positioned only six feet away in a hide in the reeds. After a long, hot wait, at just on three in the afternoon, Tibbles saw the reed warbler leave the nest. Six minutes later he heard a crashing sound in the reeds and started his camera: 'I could see a movement behind the reed warbler's nest as the cuckoo made her way forward.

As she approached the nest through the reeds she bent her head forward, right into the cup of the nest. Within seconds she raised her head and between her bill she held the egg of the reed warbler. A slight movement across the nest and she was away.'

It is during this movement that she deposits her own egg.

The cuckoo's egg conveniently hatches in twelve or thirteen days, which is usually before those of the foster-parents. Then, the rough stuff begins. Although naked and blind, the cuckoo fledgling is strangely active. On its back is a hollow patch of great sensitivity. Anything touching this seems to cause great irritation. One by one, the monstrous fledgling contrives to hoist the eggs or nestlings onto this patch and then laboriously manoeuvres them up and finally over the edge of the nest.

After each casting out the young cuckoo flops, exhausted, to the bottom of the nest, but as soon as it feels another egg or nestling touching its back, it is immediately sparked into action and repeats the process until, at last, it has the nest all to itself.

Meantime the foster-parents not only appear unmoved by the massacre, but the young cuckoo with its huge red gape induces them to work non-stop to provide it with food. After three weeks it will have increased its weight fifty times, be fully feathered and will be bulging over the nest; at this stage the foster-parents often have to stand on its back to feed it. The young cuckoo shortly leaves the nest, settling on a branch or post. Its persistent, wheezy cries and that ever-gaping bill ensure that it is fed for another week or two until it becomes more or less independent.

It was just such a young cuckoo I watched in the garden of our Suffolk cottage in early September 1975. Very strange it looked too, perched awkwardly on the low branch of a wych-elm about twenty yards away from our sitting room window. Its colouring was reddy-brown with a white spot on the head and white spots on the tail. The upper parts were barred with dark brown and the underneath was paler, barred with black. I called my wife and a neighbour and we watched it for some time. Every now and again it fluttered clumsily to the ground in search of food. My young cuckoo must have been smarter than it looked because soon it caught an earth-worm about a foot long and hoisted it in, laboriously, inch by inch.

In July or early August the adult cuckoos depart for winter

quarters in Africa leaving the young birds to make their own way, as best they can, across thousands of miles of unknown territory. Watching this inept youngster floundering about in the garden it was incredible to think that, in a week or so, it would be winging its way to Africa.

Henry Williamson wrote these notes in 1916, when he was aged nineteen, about the start of the young cuckoo's migration flight:

He will fly ten or twelve miles a day in a southerly direction. At intervals he cries in an infantile, screaming voice. There is bound to be near a pair of birds with young, and should they hear the cry, they leave their own children and go and feed the wide-mouthed imposter. No small birds, with fledglings, appear to be able to resist the call. They go and feed him. The fact that the young cuckoo bears a resemblance to a Kestrel hawk, both in flight and colour, makes their charity all the more mysterious. Down to the south he wanders, his wings getting stronger every day, until the time comes when the sea shines in the distance, and his long journey begins. And throughout the days of his English stay, he lives on the foolish and charitable ones among the smaller insectivorous birds.

[He concludes:] I have often wondered if cuckoos have the power of projecting into other birds the maternal love, or instinct, that is so obviously deficient in themselves.

Richard Jefferies, the nature writer, who greatly influenced Williamson, had expressed his opinion on this matter forty years earlier, when he wrote: 'Higher sentiments than those usually attributed to the birds and beasts of the field may, I think, be traced in some of their actions.' But I doubt if we shall ever know for certain.

It is just possible that the cuckoo is not entirely devoid of maternal feelings. J. J. Briggs Esq. wrote to the *Zoologist* in the middle of the last century to this effect:

I believe that, although confiding her young to the care of other birds, the cuckoo does not entirely forget them. I am strengthened in the opinion by a fact which fell under my notice in June 1849. As I was walking over a particular part of this parish, with a dog, I was struck with the remarkable actions of a cuckoo. It came flying about me within a hundred yards, seeming agitated and alarmed, and occasionally struck down at the dog in the same manner as the Lapwing does. It immediately occurred to me that the bird had young near, and that these actions were the result of maternal solicitude. I examined the neighbouring hedgerows in order to find the nest, but without avail. The next day a neighbouring farmer told me that he had something to show me, which proved to be a young Cuckoo in the nest of a Hedge Sparrow, and the place where the nest was situated was but a very short distance from the spot where the old Cuckoo had attracted my attention in the manner described.

F. A. Morris: extract from 'A History of British Birds'

The principal birds victimised by cuckoos are meadow pipits, dunnocks, and reed warblers, though the nests of robins, sedge warblers and pied wagtails are also favoured. In all, at one time or another, a cuckoo's egg has been found in the nests of more than fifty species. Another remarkable thing is that eggs laid by cuckoos vary in colour. Whenever possible, the bird will choose the nest of the same species that reared it and lay eggs closely resembling those of its foster-parent. Thus there is often a degree of egg mimicry, but, even when there is not, some species will still accept a cuckoo's egg as their own.

The mysteries and country legends about cuckoos seem endless: 'In June, he changes his tune.' The curious stammer may well be caused by emotion and excitement when chasing a female, rather than by the calendar. But it is most often heard in June and may be caused by the excited anticipation of migration.

Edith Simpson who lives in Yorkshire and whose poems so often neatly hit the nail on the head sums up like this:

> Why was the cuckoo ever made? –
> Did the Creator, all plans laid
> For a perfect world, draw back in doubt,
> Feeling the need for a layabout? –
> For creatures artful and worldly-wise
> To walk the earth or skim the skies
> And give to life an abrasive touch,
> Lest a perfect world be just too much?
> Profligate parent, carefree cad,
> Sign that the earth is for good and bad –
> Welcome cuckoo! – I have no doubt
> The good Lord knows what He's about.

Edith Simpson: 'It Takes All Sorts'

The Cuckoo

But perhaps that incomparable observer of the early nineteenth-century English countryside John Clare should have the final word:

> The cuckoo, like a hawk in flight,
> With narrow pointed wings
> Whews o'er our heads – soon out of sight
> And as she flies she sings:
> And darting down the hedgerow side
> She scares the little bird
> Who leaves the nest it cannot hide
> While plaintive notes are heard.
>
> I've watched it on an old oak tree
> Sing half an hour away
> Until its quick eye noticed me
> And then it whewed away.
> Its mouth when open shone as red
> As hips upon the brier,
> Like stock doves seemed its winged head
> But striving to get higher
>
> It heard me rustle and above leaves
> Soon did its flight pursue,
> Still waking summer's melodies
> And singing as it flew.
> So quick it flies from wood to wood
> 'Tis miles off 'ere you think it gone;
> I've thought when I have listening stood
> Full twenty sang – when only one.
>
> When summer from the forest starts
> Its melody with silence lies,
> And, like a bird from foreign parts,
> It cannot sing for all it tries.
> 'Cuck cuck' it cries and mocking boys
> Crie 'Cuck' and then it stutters more
> Till quick forgot its own sweet voice
> It seems to know itself no more.
>
> *John Clare (1793–1864): 'The Cuckoo'*

4

The Tawny Owl

'Tis the middle of the night by the castle clock
And the Owls have awakened the crowing cock!
Tu-whit! Tu-whit!
And hark again! the crowing cock,
How lazily he crew!
Samuel Taylor Coleridge (1772–1834): extract from 'Christabel'

There are probably very many people who have never even heard an owl, let alone seen one in the wild and yet the tawny, brown or wood owl is not uncommon and can be found close to the centre of most cities. Wherever there are woods or well-timbered parks and gardens the bird will almost certainly be found. The exceptions in Britain are: Orkney and Shetland, the Outer Hebrides and Ireland.

Owls are of course easier to hear than to see. In the trees around my Hampstead cottage they hoot spasmodically from January until the end of May and then again in the autumn. To me it is a weird though welcome sound. And yet recently, towards evening, I was passing under a fine chestnut tree when an owl hidden directly above me suddenly hooted; and for a moment my blood was chilled.

The sight or sound of an owl can be especially alarming on the rare occasions when it ventures forth by daylight. Nearly all the tawny owl's hunting is done at night, except when there are young in the nest, when it may have to do a day shift as well if hard-pressed for food. This consists mainly of mice, voles, young rats or shrews. Sometimes small birds are also taken and occasionally frogs, worms and insects. The small mammals are swallowed whole, head first, so that much of the owl's time when inactive is spent in digesting its prey.

The bones, fur, beetles' wings and other undigested materials are then regurgitated as greyish-green pellets about two inches long. These soon form quite a collection at the foot of the tree chosen as the daytime roost.

The nest itself is usually in the hole of a tree and the pure white eggs numbering from two to four are simply laid at the bottom of it without any proper nest being built. It is the female that sits on the eggs while the male does most of the hunting. If food is scarce only one or two young may be reared successfully. The young are the strangest looking creatures like little balls of grey fluff and the parents have a hectic time feeding them for it is nearly three months after leaving the nest before they are able to catch their own prey.

Tawny owls nest earlier than most birds because mice and voles are easier to find when the ground cover is sparse. As soon as the young are able to tear up the furry food for themselves, the female also goes hunting and helps the male at the difficult time when the vegetation has grown thicker.

John Clare, once himself a herd-boy, well knew the disturbing effect of an owl seen by day. In his time, early in the nineteenth century, superstitions were rife in the country and the silent, phantom-like flight of the owl must have given rise to many a ghostly legend. The spelling used here of 'white' for 'wight' is Clare's own and so is the lack of punctuation:

> The Owlet leaves her hiding place at noon
> And flaps her grey wings in the doubting light
> The hoarse jay screams to see her out so soon
> And small birds chirp and startle with affright
> Much doth it scare the superstitious white
> Who dreams of sorry luck and sore dismay
> While cow boys think the day a dream of night
> And oft grow fearful on their lonely way
> Who fancy ghosts may wake and leave their graves by day.
>
> *John Clare (1793–1864): extract from 'The Shepherd's Calendar'*

Above all, the hoot of an owl augurs winter, as Shakespeare well knew:

> When icicles hang by the wall,
> And Dick the Shepherd blows his nail;

And Tom bears logs into the hall,
And milk comes frozen home in pail;
When blood is nipp'd, and ways be foul,
Then nightly sings the staring owl,
Tu-whit, to who,
A merry note,
While greasy Joan doth keel the pot.

When all aloud the wind doth blow,
And coughing drowns the parson's saw;
And birds sit brooding in the snow,
And Marian's nose looks red and raw;
When roasted crabs hiss in the bowl,
Then nightly sings the staring owl,
Tu-whit, to-who,
A merry note,
While greasy Joan doth keel the pot.

Those lines from *Love's Labour's Lost* make me feel I want to blow on my fingers to keep the cold away too and yet Shakespeare who knew his birds well slipped up over the owl. The hoot is not the traditional 'tu-whit, to-who'. That is the sound made by a pair of owls. The male gives a long drawn-out, hollow-sounding 'hoo' followed by another wavering and slightly higher-pitched 'oooo-oooo'. Then like a whip crack in the frosty air comes 'kee-wick' from the female. This is often repeated several times and is by far the most striking sound. Both sexes can make the same calls but they are usually made by two owls in a kind of eerie duet. Shakespeare's sardonic use of the word 'merry' is sheer magic.

A traditional song also insists that the owl is quite a jolly character:

Of all the birds that ever I see,
The owl is the fairest in her degree.
For all the day long she sits in a tree,
And when the night cometh, away flies she.
To-whit! To-who! says she, To-who!
Cinamon, ginger, nutmegs and cloves,
And brandy gave me my jolly red nose.

A Celebration of Birds

The lark in the morn ascendeth on high,
And leaves the poor owl to sob and to sigh;
And all the day long, the owl is asleep,
While little birds blithely are singing, cheep! cheep!
To-whit! To-who! says she, To-who!
Cinamon, ginger, nutmegs and cloves,
And brandy gave me my jolly red nose.

There's many a brave bird boasteth awhile,
And proves himself great, let Providence smile,
Be hills and be vallies all covered with snow,
The poor owl will shiver and mock with Ho! Ho!
To-whit! To-who! says she, To-who!
Cinamon, ginger, nutmegs and cloves,
And brandy gave me my jolly red nose.

Anon.

It is because 'all the day long she sits in a tree' that the tawny owl
is so very difficult to see. For the most part it sits bolt upright with
its side pressed close against the trunk of the tree. The eyes are half-
closed, the expression bland like a cat that's stolen the cream, and
the maddening thing is that although well-nigh invisible itself every
move is being watched:

With quiet step and careful breath
we rubbered over grass and stone,
seeking that soft light-feathered bird
among the trees where it had flown.
The twisting road ran down beside
a straggling wood of ash and beech;
between us and the shadowed trees
a wire fence topped the whin-spiked ditch.
We stood and gazed: the only stir
of dry leaves in the topmost boughs;
the only noise now, far away,
the cawing of the roosting crows.
And as we watched in waning light,
our clenched attention pinned upon
that empty corner of the wood,
it seemed the quiet bird had gone.

The Tawny Owl

Then when the light had ebbed to dusk
you moved a hand and signalled me:
I saw the little pointed ears
beside a tall and narrow tree.
A further signal, and I moved
in wide half-circle to surprise
that little feathered sheaf of life
that watched you watch with steady eyes.
But when I came by easy stealth,
at last, within a yard or two
the brown bird spread enormous wings
and rose and quietly withdrew.
And we were left to carry home
a sense no mortal will devised,
that, for one instant out of time,
we had been seen and recognised.

John Hewitt

The eyes and ears of owls are indeed remarkable. As a nocturnal bird, to hunt successfully it must be able to make the most of every glimmer of light and detect the minutest sound. The eyes are huge for its size, being considerably larger than the human eye, but they are fixed in their sockets and can only look to the front. This might seem a handicap, but to compensate for the lack of eye movement the owl is able to turn his head almost full circle. No wonder when searching for an owl there is sometimes a feeling of being watched oneself. He is probably sitting motionless in a tree all the time with just his head following you slowly round until his eyes are looking backwards.

The ears too are exceptionally large, though concealed by a skin-flap, and an even stranger thing about the tawny owl's ears is that the right ear is larger than the left. This may possibly help it to pinpoint the tiny sounds made by small mammals in the dark.

The owl is wise to stay well out of sight during the day, because once he leaves his usual perch and other birds spot him he is unmercifully mobbed – jays, blackbirds, chaffinches, tits – they all gang up and give him hell. This, in fact, is the best chance you may have of seeing an owl in daylight. So, if ever there is a sudden, terrific hullabaloo from a host of small birds in a wood, then look out for an owl:

The sluggish, slothful and the dastarde Owle
Hating the day and loving of the night,
About olde sepulchres doth daily howle,
Frequenting barnes and houses without light,
And hides him often in an ivy tree,
Lest with small chattering birds he wrong'd should be.

Robert Chester: 'Love's Martyr'

The owl has been the subject of many a folk song and country rhyme. Many of these suggest the bird once knew better days. This song was known to Charles Waterton, the Yorkshire naturalist. He used to hear children singing it when he was a boy around the end of the eighteenth century:

Once I was a monarch's daughter
And sat on a lady's knee;
But am now a nightly rover,
Banished to the ivy tree,
Crying, Hoo hoo, hoo hoo, hoo hoo.
Hoo! Hoo! Hoo! My feet are cold!
Pity me, for here you see me.
Persecuted, poor and old!

Philip Gosse: 'Traveller's Rest'

As far back as about 350 B.C. the great Aristotle who was a keen observer of nature wrote about the birds of the night:

The Noctuae, Cicumae and the rest, which cannot see by day, obtain their food by seeking it at night: and yet they do not do this all night long, only at eventide and dawn. They hunt moreover mice, lizards, and scorpions, and small beasts of the like kind. All other birds flock round the Noctua, or as men say 'admire', and flying at it buffet it. Wherefore this being its nature, fowlers catch with it many and different kinds of little birds.

Aristotle's words were translated by the sixteenth-century naturalist Dr William Turner.

The Greek goddess Athene was considered to be the embodiment of wisdom and power. To her the owl was a sacred bird and even appeared on coins with Athene's head on one side and the owl upon the other. John Gay the eighteenth-century playwright and ballad writer took up his pen in sympathy with the bird's decline:

The Tawny Owl

Two formal Owls together sat,
Conferring thus in solemn chat:
How is the modern taste decay'd!
Where's the respect to wisdom paid?
Our worth the Grecian sages knew;
They gave our sires the honour due;
They weigh'd the dignity of fowls,
And pry'd into the depth of Owls.
Athens the seat of learned fame,
With gen'ral voice revered our name;
On merit, title was conferr'd,
And all adored th' Athenian Bird.

John Gay (1685–1732): 'The Two Owls and the Sparrow'

By 1850, even in Athens what a fall there had been for the owl. It took a certain determined young Englishwoman to rescue this one from a group of yelling Greek boys:

She was a small brown owl, and she had fallen out of her nest above the pillars of the Parthenon. Blinded by the sunlight, she was at the mercy of her tormentors until a stern English voice scattered them and a pair of deft English hands smoothed her ruffled feathers. The voice and the hands belonged to Miss Florence Nightingale, then sightseeing in Greece with the ever-acquiescent Mrs. Bracebridge. Adopted, invested with the appropriate name of Athena and borne over miles of land and water to a country never visited by her tutelary goddess, not even in the likeness of a sea-eagle, the little owl lived for some years at Embley, the Nightingales' home in Hampshire, where she became tame enough to be carried in a deep-pocket between the stiff, distended folds of her mistress's crinoline.

D. M. Stuart: 'A Book of Birds and Beasts'

The lady with the lump?

Nearer our own time that sensitive writer and naturalist Henry Williamson wrote of a London owl. This was in 1920:

A scolding by blackbirds, thrushes, titmice and robins awakened me one summer morning, and thinking that a mouching suburban cat had caught a bird, I sprang out of bed and peered through the open window. Eastwards the outline of Shooters Hill was dusky in the smoky haze, for the sun had not yet topped its wooded fringe. The morning star was silver-gold, and shining through the branches of the elm tree at the bottom of the garden. Two blackbirds with spread tails were perched on the fence behind, shrilling their hate at something unseen by myself. As I watched, a bird with great soft brown wings swung sideways from the tree, two dark eyes stared at me, and with feet swinging, a tawny owl sailed over the adjacent gardens, and disappeared into a shrubbery.

Williamson observed this urban owl through a winter and another spring; eventually he found the nest:

In April I heard two owls hooting, and knew that there must be a nest somewhere. Gradually I learned that the pair was well known in the district. One of the birds had been heard calling on a house roof at the same time every night; another was accustomed to perch near a mews, presumably watching for rats. An acquaintance told me that he had seen an owl dozing in the cowl of his chimney-pot, quite near the main street, where tramcars, motor-buses, and drays were always passing.

Williamson found the nest in an elm tree and wrapping his head in a coat climbed up a ladder to reach it. He brought down the two grey owlets within. One subsequently died, but the other he succeeded in rearing. In the autumn he decided to let it fly but it disappeared. Later he heard that a rag-and-bone man had captured it. Williamson tracked him to Deptford Market where he was able to buy the owl back for ten shillings and brought it back in triumph to his garden:

Clumsily it flapped to a near thorn, pursued by scolding sparrows and titmice. I called the owl, but it made as if to fly, so I withdrew, and my last sight of it was hunched angrily in the hawthorn, surrounded by sparrows. Suddenly it shot forth a foot and seized one, and twittering their terror, the other birds flew away.

I find that rather a sad story and Mr Williamson himself probably wished he had left the owlets to live their own free lives in the London jungle.

Laurie Lee wrote these haunting lines about another town owl:

On eves of cold, when slow coal fires,
rooted in basements, burn and branch,
brushing with smoke the city air;

The Tawny Owl

When quartered moons pale in the sky,
and neons glow along the dark
like deadly nightshade on a brier;

Above the muffled traffic then
I hear the owl, and at his note
I shudder in my private chair.

For like an augur he has come
to roost among our crumbling walls,
his blooded talons sheathed in fur.

Some secret lure of time it seems
has called him from his country wastes
to hunt a newer wasteland here.

And where the candelabra swung,
bright with the dancers' thousand eyes,
now his black, hooded pupils stare,

And where the silk-shoed lovers ran
with dust of diamonds in their hair,
he opens now his silent wing,

And, like a stroke of doom, drops down,
and swoops across the empty hall,
and plucks a quick mouse off the stair . . .

The country owls sometimes have a better time of it:

Sweet Suffolk Owl, so trimly dight
With feathers, like a lady bright,
Thou sing'st alone, sitting by night,
Te whit! Te whoo! Te whit! To whit!

Thy note that forth so freely rolls
With shrill command the mouse controls;
And sings a dirge for dying souls –
Te whit! Te whoo! Te whit! To whit!

Anon.

63

Unfortunately, even in the country, the owl's life is far from being a bed of roses. I think there has been a slight slackening in persecution of recent years but, traditionally, the bird has suffered simply because of its hooked beak. For many gamekeepers, that has been sufficient to condemn it. The eminent zoologist Philip Gosse protested:

It is indeed strange, and sad as well, that this constant and stupid persecution should be waged upon the farmers' and the gamekeepers' best friends, the barn and the brown or wood owl. No two birds kill more rats and mice than do these two. The number of these vermin which a pair of owls with young will destroy in a season is prodigious, and yet the majority of keepers kill any owl on sight.

Let us hope that farmers and gamekeepers will increasingly see the light and accept the evidence that can be found in the pellets. There are certainly no more harmless and useful birds; the more owls hunting on silent wings in the night the fewer rodents there will be to plague us:

> And the great brown owl flew away in her cowl,
> With her large, round shining eyes.
>
> *J. E. Browne*

5

The House Sparrow

The viewpoint of the sparrow
Is arrogant and narrow,
He *knows* that he excels,
He is selfishly obsessed;
He would not give an ostrich best.
His children leave their shells
Puffed to their very marrows
With pride at being sparrows.

So wrote Marie de la Welch and, indeed, his must be one of the greatest success stories of all time. It started thousands of years ago when man first gave up his nomadic, hunting life and turned to the cultivation of crops. The sparrow, a seed-eater with a short, powerful bill, soon got the message and lost no time in moving in on man's dwellings where easy pickings were to be found. By so doing, it neatly solved all its living problems: holes in walls and roofs provided snug nesting places and even in the hardest weather there were scraps of some kind to be had from man and from the animals he kept. Most important of all, there was no need to set out on hazardous migration flights in search of food or, alternatively, to remain behind in winter and risk starvation. 'Spuggie' had got it made.

Unfortunately, there was one inconvenience. Primitive man was not above catching and eating the odd sparrow as a change of diet and so, from hard experience over the centuries, the bird has acquired a wary, suspicious nature. While only too eager, with all the cheek in the world, to make use of man, the sparrow resents undue familiarity and is inclined to regard its benefactor with a jaundiced eye.

J. H. Gurney in his *Early Annals of Ornithology*, 1921, threw some light on this:

Small birds were not considered friends by tillers of the soil in England (in the 15th century), and it was the custom for boys to be sent into the fields with bows and arrow, which with the help of some shouting, were expected to scare all such thieves away. Then, as now, the parasitical House Sparrow, whether a native or not, knew well how to thrive upon man's labour. No one can prove from where the sparrow originally sprung, but a robber of grain it has been from the earliest times, and in proof of this indictment may be cited an illustration in the 'Hortus Sanitatis'. This 'Hortus' which was a medical treatise of the fifteenth century (printed 1485 and 1491) sometimes with coloured pictures, depicts four sparrows attacking a field of ripe corn, probably real sparrows, but it has to be remembered that the term was used in a generic sense . . . The House Sparrow was establishing itself, and was already honoured with a nick-name – Phyllyp Sparrowe. 'The Boke of Phyllyp Sparrowe', written by a native of Norfolk (Master John Skelton, 1508) . . . brings in the names of sixty-nine birds . . .

The tenant must have been very poor who could render no higher rent than common Sparrows, but in July 1533, in default of anything better, twelve 'sparouse' are accepted, and in the same week there also comes 'twelve sparouse, three herns', the latter probably nestlings, for which three halfpence is allowed. The Sparrows also, judging from the time of year, may have been young ones.

In July 1548, Mr. le Strange finds two dozen more Sparrows, and two dozen more in September, presumably for eating, as they could hardly have been bought for any other purpose, unless it was to feed the hawks.

That same Master Skelton suggests that the bird even featured on the menu in the holiest of places. Carrow was a nunnery in a suburb of Norwich, founded in 1146:

> For the soul of Philip Sparrow
> That was late slain at Carrow
> Among the Nunnes Black,
> For that sweet soules sake
> And for all sparrows' Souls
> Set in our bread-rolls,
> *Pater noster qui*
> With an *Ave Mari.*
>
> *John Skelton (1460–1529): 'The Sparrow's Dirge'*

So perhaps it's not surprising that the sparrow is so much on his guard – after all, who wants to end up in a bread-roll?

John Clare, the Northamptonshire farm-labourer poet was quick to come to the bird's defence:

> Sure my sparrows are my own,
> Let ye then my birds alone.
> Come poor birds, from foes severe
> Fearless come, you're welcome here:
> My heart yearns at fate like yours,
> A sparrow's life's as sweet as ours.
> Hardy clowns! grudge not the wheat
> Which hunger forces birds to eat:
> Your blinded eyes, worst foes to you,
> Can't see the good which sparrows do.
> Did not poor birds with watching rounds
> Pick up the insects from your grounds,
> Did they not tend your rising grain,
> You then might sow to reap in vain.
>
> *John Clare (1793–1864): extract from*
> *'To Boys not to Kill the Sparrows on his Roof'*

The eighteenth-century poet William Cowper was an acute observer of birdlife and he knew about the flocks of sparrows descending like locusts on the grain and had seen the hedgers trying to scare them with their bows and arrows:

> The sparrow, meanest of the feathered race,
> His fit companion finds in every place,
> With whom he filches the grain that suits him best,
> Flits here and there, and late returns to rest;
> And whom if chance the falcon makes his prey,
> Or hedger with his well-aimed arrow slay,
> In no such loss the gay survivor grieves,
> New love he seeks, and new delight receives.

Cowper is implying that the sparrow is a faithless creature; another writer, his contemporary, Charles Churchill, took a different view:

> Like sparrow who, depriv'd of mate,
> Snatch'd by the cruel hand of fate,
> From spray to spray no more will hop,
> But sits alone on the house-top.

Somehow, I doubt whether a sparrow would sit alone for very long on a house-top or anywhere else for that matter. It always seeks the company of its kind even if for no higher reason than that when one or two are gathered together there is a better chance of easy pickings. Greed in fact seems to be its greatest drive and a determination that none shall fare better than itself. A sparrow will even covet the branch to which another sparrow is clinging.

The town bird is about as nondescript in appearance as it is possible to be:

> In busy mart and crowded street,
> There the smoke-brown sparrow sits.
>
> *Eliza Cook (1818–1889)*

But see a cock bird in the country in spring and what a difference. He is then quite a handsome bird with his brown upper parts streaked with black, a distinguished grey crown and glossy black bib. The female, in comparison, is rather drab – just a little brown bird with streaks on her back.

Drab to us perhaps, but to a cock sparrow no doubt she's a wow. This is demonstrated at courtship parties. A single cock bows to a hen, chirping loudly the while. In no time, other cocks muscle in and noisy scuffles become the order of the day. The female soon departs, leaving her suitors chirping and squabbling. As soon as they discover she has gone, the chase is on and the whole gang goes in hot pursuit. In these mating battles 'spuggie' takes a keen and near-constant interest.

Once a pair is formed, the male does most of the nest building and a rough old job he makes of it too. An untidy tangle of straw and rubbish piled into a crevice under the eaves or straggling from behind a drainpipe.

Once the site has been chosen, the same nest is used year after year; its appearance becoming ever stragglier. This I know to my cost as, a few years back, a pair made their abode in a thick clump of clematis growing just outside the bedroom window in Hamp-

stead. They seem to be exceptionally hysterical sparrows and, especially when there are young in the nest, keep up a constant 'cheep-cheeping' from daybreak to nightfall. The stupid part about it is that there is no need for all the excitement as they have chosen the safest site imaginable. As they have at least three broods a year, my wife and I will just have to get used to the sound. In the words of the Psalmist: 'Yea, the sparrow hath found her an house.'

It is curious that when, owing to a shortage of housing accommodation, the sparrow has to nest in a hedgerow or bush he is perfectly capable of building a large, quite splendid, domed structure, but presumably only does this because in that situation more warmth and protection is required.

Being assured of a steady food supply from man's activities, has meant comparative freedom for the sparrow from the drudgery of constant foraging. It has more time than other birds to loaf around; more time to sharpen up its wits. Psychologists in America have carried out tests making use of a maze. These showed that the house sparrow has about the same level of intelligence as a white rat or a monkey. He is certainly among the most intelligent of birds.

Viscount Grey of Fallodon in his book *The Charm of Birds* gives a typical instance of the way a sparrow never misses a trick:

There has lately been an instance at Fallodon of the cleverness of sparrows. It has been the custom for several years to keep a basket of bread in the greenhouse, that it may be at hand to feed the waterfowl. More than one pair of chaffinches nest near the greenhouse, but they have never discovered the bread. Three years ago a pair of sparrows nested in the garden. There had been none there for some time after horses were no longer kept. It did not take these sparrows long, though their nest was fifty yards away, to discover the bread, and how to get in and out of the greenhouse through the top ventilator. The moment anyone entered they flew out at the top, without losing their way. The neighbouring chaffinches have not made the discovery, not even since the sparrows came and showed the way. Yet chaffinches are as fond as sparrows of feeding their young with soft bread.

Many townspeople might also consider it the most numerous of birds, but this is only true of built-up areas. Taking Britain overall, the house sparrow is in fact outnumbered by the chaffinch and the blackbird. I don't believe there are anything like as many sparrows as in my early boyhood of the twenties. Then, horses were still widely used for deliveries of all kinds.

Our house in the Surrey suburb of Croydon was at the top of a steep hill. Daily, the chariot-like milk-float would toil its way up, the horse meandering from left to right and back again across the crown of the road to avoid the straight pull to the top. There was so little traffic in those days. I remember too the dashing butcher's cart with its high-stepping pony, the lumbering coal wagons and brewers' drays – a great clatter of horses daily providing the richest of pickings for the ubiquitous sparrows. How they must mourn the loss of their four-footed providers.

On the other hand, taking the world as a whole, it must certainly be one of the most widely distributed species. New fields of conquest were opened up in the second half of the last century when the sparrow was introduced to North and South America, to say nothing of Australia and New Zealand. How 'spuggie' must have gloated as he grabbed at his new opportunities. In America these came in the shape of worms. *Animal World* of 1 October 1869 carried a somewhat optimistic, not to say ingenuous report:

In the large American cities, especially like those of Philadelphia, that have their streets lined with shade-trees, a great want is felt in the scarcity of insectivorous birds. Insect life overruns us in summer; the shade-trees are destroyed by a species of worm known as the 'span-worm' or measuring worm, and these insects, hanging on their long silken cords from the trees in large numbers, get on clothes of passengers and, especially for timorous persons, render a walk along the sidewalk a disagreeable task. These worms have been growing in numbers during late seasons, owing to the want of insect-eating birds, and finally the city government has taken the matter in hand and gone to the mother country for a remedy. An agent was sent to England to collect 1,000 sparrows, who arrived at Ashton about Christmas, and filled his commission there, employing lads to catch the birds, and paying them 2½d to 4d apiece. The birds were caged and brought to this city, and taken care of until the spring opened, and a few days ago were liberated in the heart of the city to fly whither they chose. They have since been seen building nests in belfries and under the eaves of buildings, and have also taken possession of boxes set up for them in parks and squares, and are expected to multiply rapidly, and be in good condition to fight the enemy when he arrives two or three months hence. The immigrants have received a warm welcome from the city. The Mayor, in a special proclamation issued at the time of their liberation, enjoins all persons from injuring them, and requests the public to protect them; and the Philadelphia Society for the Prevention of Cruelty to Animals has taken the little strangers under its especial care.

Those little strangers wasted no time in taking over, as becomes clear from an editorial appearing in *Country Life*, 11 September 1897. This is how the writer assessed the house sparrow's impact on its new home:

The history of his eminent success in America is one of the most interesting chapters in natural history, analogous to that which treats of the disastrous importation of the rabbit into Australia. Originally taken to America to clear the Madison Square trees of some caterpillar plague with which the native insectivorous birds were not able to cope, he not only accomplished that original purpose, but remained on the land, multiplied and overspread it, eating of everything, and of corn apparently by preference, until he allowed the native American birds to remain in their haunts only on sufferance and after much battle. And this pugnacity of his, in addition to his voracity, is one of the counts in the indictment that Miss Ormerod and Mr. Tegetmeier bring against him in his native home. Doubtless it is his only too British habit to deem his natural enemy any other bird that crosses his path. Song birds and insect-eating birds, he chases them all away, by the might of the strong beak. Often, when a pair of house martins have built themselves, with much pains, their adobe residence under the eaves, we see sticking from it ragged ends of straw and hay. This, it is very certain, is not part of the domestic economy of the martins. It is the furniture – the tenants' fixtures – of the sparrow, who has remorselessly ousted the original owners and occupies their home and hearth.

The sparrow is of the same mind as W. C. Fields: 'Never give a sucker an even break.'

Apart from ousting the delightful martins, the sparrow has other little ways that do nothing to endear him to gardeners. For his dust-bath, what better than a choice seed-bed? Then there is its infuriating habit of wantonly attacking crocus petals, especially when yellow. Polyanthus flowers are also sometimes savaged and nobody seems to know why. I rather think sparrows eat the pollen, as I have sometimes spotted them pecking at the stamens of the flowers.

Another interesting problem is how to prevent them from hogging all the food put out on bird-tables and intended for more decorative and timid species. There is no golden rule about this. It is simply a question of pitting one's wits against the sparrow in any local situation.

Probably, the containers it finds most difficult to raid are the wooden ones that can be hung on a branch and where it can only gain access by clinging upside down to the underneath. For tits and nuthatches this is no problem whereas the sparrows do find it rather taxing. But, after a crash-course, they usually get the knack. It's not easy to defeat them – the only way is to keep on trying.

And yet most townsmen at least would probably miss the cheekiness and audacity of the sparrow. He always comes up smiling. Thomas Hardy wrote of him in 'Snow in the Suburbs':

> A sparrow enters the tree.
> Whereon immediately
> A snow-lump thrice his own slight size
> Descends on him and showers his head and eyes,
> And overturns him
> And near inurns him.

The poet Stephen Duck noted how sparrows rush for cover in rain:

> Thus have I seen, on a bright summer's day,
> On some green brake, a flock of sparrows play;
> From twig to twig, from bush to bush they fly,
> And with continued chirping fill the sky:
> But, on a sudden, if a storm appears,
> Their chirping noise no longer dins your ears;
> They fly for shelter to the thickest bush;
> There silent sit, and all at once is hush.

And let us not forget the sparrow's value as a destroyer of insect pests during the summer months when it greatly helps keep the roses clear of aphids and then goes on to clean up the caterpillars. A writer in *Cannel's Floral Guide* of 1870 gave this tip to his readers: 'Caterpillars are very troublesome towards the Autumn, and I find the best preventative is to feed the sparrows near where the choice geraniums grow, and they will keep them cleaner than your looking them over every other day.'

In spite of all its wariness and suspicion, a sparrow can be tamed. John Clare kept a pet one for three years:

The common sparrow is well known but not so much in a domesticated state as few people think it worth while bringing up a sparrow. When I was a boy I kept a tamed cock sparrow 3 years. It was so tame that it would come when called and flew where it pleased. When I first had the sparrow I was fearful of the cat killing it, so I used to hold the bird in my hand toward her and when she attempted to smell of it I beat her. She at last would take no notice of it and I ventured to let it loose in the house. They were both very shy of each other at first, and when the sparrow ventured to chirp, the cat would brighten up as if she intended to seize it but she went no further than a look or smell. At length she had kittens and when they were taken away, she grew so fond of the sparrow as to attempt to caress it. The sparrow was startled at first but came to by degrees and ventured so far at last as to perch upon her back. Puss would call for it when out of sight like a kitten and would lay mice before it the same as she would for her own young. They always lived in harmony, so much so that the sparrow would often take away bits of bread from under the cat's nose and even put itself in a posture of resistance when offended as if it reckoned her no more than one of its kind. In winter when we could not bear the door open to let the sparrow come out and in, I was allowed to take a pane out of the window, but in the spring of the third year my poor Tom Sparrow – for that was the name he was called by – went out and never returned. I went day after day calling out for Tom and eagerly eyeing every sparrow on the house, but none answered the name, for he would come down in a moment to the call and perch upon my hand to be fed. I gave it out that some cat which it mistook for its old favourite betrayed its confidence and destroyed it.

John Clare (1793–1864): 'Sparrows' extract from 'The Prose of John Clare'

Another charming story of a tame sparrow appeared in *Country Life* on 30 March 1901. The writer was a maid in service with a Mrs Hervey of Beechfield, Alderley Edge in Cheshire. Her name was Clara A. Beasley and she was engaged to look after Mrs Hervey's little daughter Marjorie. Her duties cannot have been unduly arduous as she had time to write:

We were going for a walk one evening last July, when Miss Marjorie found a tiny bird lying on the ground close to the house. It had evidently just been hatched, and must have fallen from a considerable height, as the nearest nest was in a pipe which runs round the roof of the house. We

74

Plates: **1 Tawny Owl 2 Robin and young
3 Blue tit and Great tit 4 Cuckoo**

4

decided to try to keep it and, having gained permission from Mrs. Hervey to do so, we found a quill, fed our pet with bread and milk, and placed it in a nest of cotton wool. We did not then think it could possibly live many minutes. Our astonishment was therefore very great to find, when we returned from our walk, that it was not only alive but very bright, and quite satisfied with its surroundings.

I took it to my room that night and, in answer to its cries, fed it two or three times during the night. From that time it grew very quickly, and could hop and fly short distances, being covered with a little coat of brown feathers, and so betraying that he came of very common parentage. But the word common could not be applied to our wee birdie. From the very first day he was with us he carefully studied our words and the expressions of our faces, and soon grew to understand both, and, from the day he could fly about, entered into every detail of our human life with an energy and intelligence that at times would startle us, so very unnatural did it seem to us.

When the room was warm, birdie was most particular about his bath, and was so vain that he would not show himself until his little coat was dry and neatly arranged.

Birdie's chief point of observation was from my shoulder. Often when sewing he would fly to my finger and, holding the point of the needle in his tiny beak, endeavour to draw it from the work and, failing this, would set to work to pull out all the previous stitches. He would fly away with needles, buttons and hooks, and carefully hide them. He soon learnt his way about the house and when we went to any of the rooms would quickly come in search of us and, on finding us, would fly to our shoulders, fluttering his little wings and chirping with great pleasure and excitement.

He was extremely fond of lace and jewellery, and would critically examine any new thing, expressing either approval or disgust. Often he would stand over a thing and fight most bravely for its possession, even keeping three of us at bay; and often at meals he would eat from our plates, but would eat nothing laid upon the table-cloth.

We have a canary in the nursery, which whistles most sweetly, and so well could birdie imitate him that not the slightest difference could be detected. He soon changed his first coat of feathers for a very pretty one – it was a very glossy shaded brown, with grey and black breast and grey feathers on either side. Birdie managed to fly away through the nursery window three times, twice returning of his own accord after being away two hours. But the third time, after sitting near the window for some time, he flew away to the orchard, and when night came he had not returned, and our efforts to find him were in vain.

Early the next morning I went down to the orchard, and called him by name, when to my great astonishment he flew to my shoulder, and expressed the greatest delight at being found.

Birdie's death occurred on January 13th. The children and I were playing with a toy train, and as usual birdie came to give us his assistance. How the accident occurred, no one can say but, chancing to turn a moment, we saw our wee pet stagger and fall. Carefully we raised him, but all our efforts to save him were in vain; in three minutes he died.

Throughout his life he never expressed the slightest fear, and so in the last moments he gave no sign of the pain through which he passed, only when the brief struggle was over raised his tiny head, gave us one last bright look, as though he fully realised our deep sorrow, and with one cry of farewell fell back lifeless. Birdie, our sweet little companion, was gone, and all that remains to us are the sweetest memories and a silent little figure, which now stands on a cabinet in the nursery, watching with calm indifference all those actions which once could not have proceeded without his tiny help.

It is quite evident then that 'spuggie' has a way with him. Even the Roman poet Catullus, who wrote those elegant lyrics to Lesbia, sang his praises:

> Sparrow, my Lesbia's darling pet,
> Her playmate whom she loves to let
> Perch in her bosom and then tease
> With tantalising fingertips,
> Provoking angry little nips
> (For my bright beauty seems to get
> A kind of pleasure from these games,
> Even relief, this being her way
> I think, of damping down the flames
> Of Passion), I wish I could play
> Silly games with you too, to ease
> My worries and my miseries.
>
> *(Translation by James Michie)*

We can't be certain that Lesbia's bird really was a sparrow because the latin word 'passer' was used for many other birds too: even the ostrich brought to strut in the Roman arena with crimson-painted plumes was known as the 'passer marinus'. Anyway, when the bird died, Catullus tells us how Lesbia mourned her playfellow:

The House Sparrow

Graces and cupids, weep and gather near,
Weep, all ye mortals that love lovely things:
Dead is the darling sparrow of my Dear.
More than her eyes she loved him. Sweet was he.
As a maid knows her mother he knew her,
And never was he fain to quit her knee.
Yet he would flutter round and pipe his lay:
For her alone he piped, his sovereign Queen.
Now must he fare along the sunless way,
Now must he journey to that dwelling dim
Whence – as too well men know – none comes again.
Woe upon Orchus' night that ravished him!
Alas, poor little sparrow, for whom being dead
My Dear has wept until her eyes are red.

(Translation by D. M. Stuart)

The eighteenth-century wit Matthew Green had a distinctly ironical turn of mind. Fair Lucia loved her sparrow but, in the end, loved her diamond more:

I lately saw, what now I sing,
Fair Lucia's hand display'd;
The finger grac'd a diamond ring,
On that a sparrow play'd.

The feather'd play-thing she caressed,
She stroked its head and wings;
And while it nestled on her breast,
She lisped the dearest things.

With chisell'd bill a spark ill-set
He loosened from the rest,
And swallowed down to grind his meat,
The easier to digest.

She seized his bill with wild affright,
Her diamond to descry:
'Twas gone! she sickened at the sight,
Moaning her bird would die.

The tongue-tied knocker none might use,
The curtains none undraw,
The footmen went without their shoes
The street was laid with straw.

The doctor used his oily art
Of strong emetic kind,
Th'apothecary played his part
And engineered behind.

When physic ceased to spend its store,
To bring away the stone,
Dicky, like people given o'er,
Picks up when let alone.

His eyes dispelled their sickly dews,
He pecked behind his wing,
Lucia, recovering at the news,
Relapses for the ring.

Meanwhile within her beauteous breast
Two different passions strove;
When av'rice ended the contest,
And triumphed over love.

Poor, little, pretty, fluttering thing,
Thy pains the sex display,
Who, only to repair a ring,
Could take thy life away.

Drive av'rice from your hearts, ye fair,
Monster of foulest mien:
Ye would not let it harbour there,
Could but its form be seen.

It made a virgin put on guile,
Truth's image break her word,
A Lucia's face forbear to smile,
A Venus kill her bird.
Matthew Green (1696–1737): 'The Sparrow and the Diamond'

Closer to our own time Bryan Waller Procter, a solicitor and friend of Leigh Hunt, Charles Lamb, Hazlitt and Dickens, wrote under the pseudonym Barry Cornwall and here probably expresses the feelings of most city dwellers:

The House Sparrow

Touch not the little sparrow who doth build
His home so near us. He doth follow us
From spot to spot amidst the turbulent town,
And ne'er desert us. To all other birds
The woods suffice, the rivers, the sweet fields,
And nature in her aspect mute and fair,
But he doth herd with man. Blithe servant! live
Feed, and grow cheerful!

And Francis Ledwidge, an Irish peasant poet who was killed in the First World War, had kind things to say:

There is no bird half so harmless,
None so sweetly rude as you,
None so common and so charmless,
None of virtues nude as you.

But for all your faults I love you,
For you linger with us still,
Though the wintry winds reprove you
And the snow is on the hill.

Francis Ledwidge: from 'To a Sparrow'

A final tribute from that great nineteenth-century American nature writer Henry David Thoreau:

I once had a sparrow alight on my shoulder for a moment while I was hoeing in a village garden, and I felt that I was more distinguished by that circumstance than I should have been by any epaulet I could have worn.

6

The Blackbird

The ousel-cock so black of hue
With orange-tawny bill,

Who but Shakespeare could have given such a magical description
of a blackbird? No wonder Bottom in his ass's head, singing to keep
his courage up in the moonlit woods when all his friends had fled,
was able to charm Titania with his song.

It is the jewel-like colour of the bill, contrasting with the matt
sable of his plumage that makes the cock blackbird such a joy to
behold. Best of all, see him against a snow-covered lawn in pale
sunshine. How fortunate we are in Britain that the blackbird with
his elegant looks and beauty of song should be among the commonest of all our birds. And it is no wonder that he has been the
subject of legend.

One of the early Christian monks St Kevin is portrayed in images
throughout Ireland as holding a blackbird in his outstretched hand.
The story goes:

At one Lenten season, St. Kevin, as was his way, fled from the company of
men to a certain solitude, and in a little hut that did but keep out the sun
and the rain, gave himself earnestly to reading and to prayer, and his
leisure to contemplation alone. And as he knelt in his accustomed fashion,
with his hand outstretched through the window and lifted up to heaven, a
blackbird settled on it, and busying herself as in her nest, laid in it an egg.
And so moved was the saint that in all patience and gentleness he remained, neither closing nor withdrawing his hand: but until the young
ones were fully hatched he held it out unwearied, shaping it for the purpose.
Translated from the Latin by Helen Waddell: 'Beasts and Saints'

The Blackbird

A saintly action indeed, but blackbirds although shy certainly do have trusting natures and their confidence can be won. Any gardener will know how a blackbird, rivalled only by the robin, will soon follow every turn of the spade.

A remarkable instance of intelligence and trust in man came from a Mr B. Baise of Wellbrook House, Mayfield, Sussex. Most days he worked in the garden with his old dog by his side, so the birds had got used to him. On 28 May 1921, he wrote:

Whilst busy digging a few days ago, with an old retriever lying close by, my attention was attracted by the behaviour of a hen blackbird towards the dog. After a casual glance I went on with my work, but soon stopped again to notice the persistent noise and behaviour of the bird.

The dog was looking bored and seemed perplexed and disturbed, for he got up and lay down again further away. The blackbird then paid its attentions to me, carried on the same performance by running towards me instead of the dog; stopping close by, opening its bill and uttering a plaintive cry; then running away some distance, always in the same direction. I thought perhaps it wanted a worm so threw it one or two, but these it utterly ignored. I then came to the conclusion that there must be some good reason for its strange behaviour, so sticking my spade in the ground I followed the bird. As soon as it saw me doing so its excitement seemed to grow. When I reached the orchard it flew into an apple-tree, and called as loudly as it could. On looking up I saw another blackbird (a male) partially hanging and very much spent. As the helpless victim was out of my reach, I went to get a short ladder, and so find out the trouble. Whilst I was gone the hen bird remained with its mate, never ceasing its plaintive cry. On reaching the helpless bird I found that one leg was tightly wedged in a ragged end of a splintered bough. With little difficulty I released the sufferer and, on examining the limb, found it unbroken. When I let him go he flew away somewhat weakly, accompanied by his clever little mate. This episode, which goes far to prove the intelligence of wild birds, I am not likely to forget, nor the wonderful way that blackbird *made* me understand it wanted my services.

Blackbirds and cats are, of course, deadly enemies and the birds will sometimes try to enlist humans as allies. This conflict was no doubt much more important to the blackbird than the Great War across the Channel. B. Balfour-Melville on 18 September 1915, picked up his pen to write:

There was a time when our suburban garden was much infested by cats, to the great disgust of the birds. When we heard the well-known cry of expostulation from the blackbirds, we and the dogs used to run to the rescue and chase away the intruders. So often this happened that at last the dogs would, without our intervention, answer the appeal, and rush with tumult from the house to find the enemy when they heard the particular note of alarm. One day my sister was walking in the garden when she heard a blackbird telling her that danger was near. She followed the call till the bird showed her a cat sound asleep on the roof of an outhouse. When this momentarily harmless foe was dislodged, the call continued and the bird led my sister for some distance to a plantation, where another cat was found sound asleep, also among the bushes. This cat being disposed of, the bird was quite content. We were immensely flattered to find that our small friends realized and appealed to our power and willingness to help them. They were absolutely *wild* birds, not pensioners.

Those cats were evidently caught on a bad wicket. Here a blackbird becomes the avenger. Frances Scripps wrote on 30 August 1919 of the action on another part of the front – Bexhill. The eye-witness was a neighbour of his:

One morning in the spring she heard loud and unusual sounds proceeding from the garden. On investigating the cause she discovered that her cat had seized and killed a hen blackbird and was gloating over her victim. But her triumph was short-lived, for in a few minutes the bird's mate flew down, and alighting on the head of the destroyer of its domestic happiness, pecked her furiously, at the same time uttering piercing cries of rage. The effect of the onslaught on the cat was remarkable. She seemed paralysed with fear, and crouched trembling during the whole time her punishment lasted – about ten minutes. When at last the bird, exhausted, flew away, the cat darted into the house and hid under a bed in one of the upper rooms. For several days afterwards she could not be persuaded to enter the garden, and when at length she ventured she looked furtively round, and both on that occasion and whenever she went into the garden in future was always on the watch for her injured and indignant enemy. If she saw or heard him she invariably rushed terror-stricken into the house. Surely this must be a rare instance of fearlessness on the part of the bird towards its inveterate foe, and fear on the part of the cat towards a creature which it holds as a rule in contempt and looks upon as its rightful prey.

H. J. Massingham: from 'Dogs, Birds, and Others'

A clear case of the biter bit. There are countless instances recorded

of the blackbird's courage in the face of the enemy; and yet there are few birds with more cautious natures. Not a strong flyer, he never likes to be far from cover, where thanks to his dark, protective colouring he feels secure. He takes immense pride in his black plumage; on alighting, jauntily switching his tail upwards. The tail also plays an important part in quarrels, and in courtship when it is flaunted and carried outspread like a fan.

There is no noisier bird in the garden or hedgerow and in spring and early summer even the mildest disturbance sets off his peculiar chuckle of alarm. Should a cat be lurking or an owl be seen, he will become positively neurotic with incessant, metallic, 'chinking' cries. Again, when roosting, he will 'chink' away for minutes at a time with no apparent reason. It were as though he took upon himself the role of sentinel for all the birds.

But exasperating as the blackbird can be at times, all is forgiven for the slow, meditative beauty of his song, perhaps best heard on a bright April evening after rain:

> It seems wrong that out of this bird,
> Black, bold, a suggestion of dark
> Places about it, there yet should come
> Such rich music, as though the notes'
> Ore were changed to a rare metal
> At one touch of that bright bill.
>
> You have heard it often, alone at your desk
> In a green April, your mind drawn
> Away from its work by sweet disturbance
> Of the mild evening outside your room.
>
> A slow singer, but loading each phrase
> With history's overtones, love, joy
> And grief learned by his dark tribe
> In other orchards and passed on
> Instinctively as they are now,
> But fresh always with new tears.
>
> *R. S. Thomas (1913–): 'A Blackbird Singing'*

Richard Jefferies was another who loved the blackbird – 'The King of the Hedge', but he liked best to listen to him in the heat of mid-summer:

The Blackbird

On a warm June day, when the hedges are covered with roses and the air is sweet with the odour of mown grass, it is pleasant to listen to the blackbirds in the oaks pouring forth their rich liquid notes. There is no note so sweet and deep and melodious as that of the blackbird to be heard in our fields; it is even richer than the nightingale's though not so varied.

Jefferies also remarks on the slowness of the song:

He sings in a quiet, leisurely way, as a great artist should: there is no haste, no notes thickening on notes in swift crescendo. His voice (so to speak) drops from him without an effort, and it is so clear that it may be heard at a long distance. It is not a set song; perhaps, in strict language, it is hardly a song at all, but rather a succession of detached notes with intervals between.

Richard Jefferies (1848–1887): 'Wild Life in a Southern County'

Or is the blackbird heard at his best at dawn, when all around is still, as though in suspense:

Then, without a murmur of warning, a spirit seems to move through the garden and before the listener is properly aware, the first notes of the chorus have stolen out into the grey, meditative silence. They are sung by thrushes in the blossom-laden apple trees, drowsily at first, but gathering in number and volume as the minutes advance. Through them, like drops of molten gold, flow the glorious, mellow phrases of blackbirds, announcing, as it were, the theme of the symphony, until every bush and tree seems to sway in the flood of song and quiver with tremulous rapture.

Anon.

I don't think the dawn chorus made any great impression on me until, as a young man, I became infatuated with a bewitching young creature of seventeen. To my delight, I was able to wangle an invitation to stay at her parents' house for a weekend in May. As an incurable romantic, to be under the same roof at night, and yet a world away, meant inevitably a sleepless night – 'une nuit blanche'. Then, before first light, the birds started: first a few sleepy, tentative notes, but building up into a full-throated pæan of praise – a tapestry of sound from a myriad voices – a great symphony of joy.

It mocked my sleepless melancholy. So I rose before the sun and walked through beechwoods where bluebells hung heavy with dew.

Why do they sing so at dawn? Perhaps as some experts say it is just a good way for birds, which are highly territorial, to find out what is going on around them. But nothing will convince me that it is not also a spontaneous explosion of joy. T. E. Brown certainly thought so:

Just Listen!

Just listen to the blackbird – what a note
The creature has! God bless his happy throat!
He is so absolutely glad
I fear he will go mad.

T. E. Brown (1830–1897): extract

In fact, the blackbird's song at dawn is often half-hearted and shrill compared with its performance later in the day.

Again T. E. Brown in his poem 'Vespers' captures perfectly the mood of the evening song:

O Blackbird, what a boy you are!
How you do go it!
Blowing your bugle to that one sweet star –
How you do blow it!
And does she hear you, blackbird boy, so far?
Or is it wasted breath?
'Good Lord! she is so bright
Tonight!'
The blackbird saith.

Another evening poem came from the pen of John Drinkwater. The blackbird works his magic too among suburban chimney pots:

He comes on chosen evenings
My blackbird bountiful, and sings
Over the gardens of the town
Just at the hour the sun goes down.
His flight across the chimneys thick,
By some divine arithmetic,
Comes to his customary stack,
And couches there his plumage black,
And there he lifts his yellow bill

The Blackbird

Kindled against the sun, till
These suburbs are like Dymock woods
Where music has her solitudes.
And while he mocks the winter's wrong
Rapt on his pinnacle of song.
Figured above our garden plots
Those are celestial chimney-pots.

John Drinkwater (1882–1937): 'He Comes on Chosen Evenings'

And who better than a blackbird to plead in song for Mary Magdalen?

Magdalen at Michael's gate,
  Tirled at the pin;
On Joseph's thorn sang the blackbird,
  'Let her in! Let her in!'

'Hast thou seen the wounds?' said Michael,
  'Knowest thou thy sin?'
'It is evening, evening, evening,
  Let her in! Let her in!'

'I have seen the wounds,' she answered,
  'And I know my sin!'
'She knows it well, well,' sang the blackbird,
  'Let her in! Let her in!'

'Thou bring'st no offering,' said Michael,
  'Nought save sin'.
And the blackbird sang, 'She is sorry,
  sorry, sorry,
  Let her in! Let her in!'

When he had sung himself to sleep,
  And night did begin,
God came and opened Michael's gate,
  And Magdalen went in.

Henry Kingsley (1830–1876): 'An Anthology for Animal Lovers'

His song is heard usually from February to July and it is in February that the serious business of courtship and nest building gets under way. Once formed, a pair usually stays together for life. Both birds set about the job of prospecting for a site, though the female shows greater determination. The nest might be almost anywhere. I heard of one in the cabin of an RAF 'V' Bomber; another under the engine cover of a cement-mixer, but most often they are in a bush or bramble a few feet above the ground. Blackbirds also favour garden sheds, garages, outhouses – anywhere they can find a ledge. This leads to problems, unless the birds can find entry and exit points other than by the door: not everyone likes to leave a door at night unlocked.

No one knew better than John Clare the surprises a blackbird can spring. Here is the true rustic voice; and freedom from punctuation:

> The blackbird has a thousand whims
> In choosing places for her nest
> In spots that so unlikely seems
> As want of skill and hardly taste
> Upon the bindings of the hedge
> On water grains of high oak tree
> In roots o'er looked by kecks and sedge
> On thorns where every eye may see.
>
> And on a gatepost's very top
> O'erhung with boughs will wonder stare
> To find them – shepherds laughing stop
> And think that boys have placed it there
> On woodstacks in a cottage yard
> Nay shelved upon an hovel stone
> I've marked them with a strange regard
> As nests some foreign birds might own.
>
> My wonder I could scarce conceal
> And what surprised me more than all
> Between the spokes of an old wheel
> That leaned against an hovel wall
> Some moss was seen; I thought it laid
> By boys to make each other stare
> But bye and bye a nest was made
> And eggs like fairy gifts were there.
>
> *John Clare (1793–1864): 'The Blackbird'*

An even greater surprise was in store for a Mr W. T. Collier who wrote from Bagley Wood, near Oxford, in May 1907:

A fortnight ago I had occasion to move some brushwood in the garden. In doing so I discovered a blackbird's nest with no eggs in, which, unfortunately, had to be moved also. On 30th April as I passed near the place I noticed a blackbird fly away, and looking down I saw three eggs lying together on the ground, partly hidden by some brushwood. The bird had apparently been sitting on the eggs for some time. There was no attempt at a nest.

Normally the female does nearly all the building work and the one that Alec Robertson, the East Anglian naturalist, observed from a hide became distinctly bossy:

The hen did practically all the work, gathering dead grass stems from just the other side of the hide-cover and picking them over with elaborate care until she found one that was exactly right. She made very heavy weather of the short flight to the bush and the journey through the foliage, flapping like an agitated chicken, and making so much noise as she barged her way round the nest to weave the grass into the structure that one might have imagined that a big dog was forcing its way through the undergrowth. The cock only once brought in a contribution, in the shape of a dead leaf, and they immediately had a tug-of-war over it, which the hen won. She placed it on the nest and then pecked and scolded until he flew off, which he did with the air of one who has made his gesture of domesticity and is only too happy to return to the club. The hen worked hard, and would take but two or three minutes to work the dead grass into the nest; within twenty-four hours the plastering had begun and in three days it was complete. Then, as so often happens among birds, there was an interval of a week before she began to lay.

A. W. P. Robertson: 'Birds Wild and Free'

The hen lays one egg a day usually in the early morning; the clutch size varies from three to five. After about a fortnight, the nestlings emerge and are fed by both parents for another hectic two weeks. The fledglings then flutter uncertainly from the safety of the nest and at this time are highly vulnerable, either from marauding cats or other predators or sometimes even from well-meaning two-legged rescuers.

In most cases when young birds are found, apparently abandoned, it is best to leave them where they are, as in time the parent birds nearly always return and feed them much better than humans can. On the other hand when a small bird is heard calling despairingly for days it is clear that help is needed.

It was just such a case W. H. Hudson wrote of in his Hampshire garden. The problem was to know how best to help. For half an hour he tried to catch it but the youngster always managed to avoid him by fluttering away feebly under the brambles. Scraps left out for him were not taken. Hudson then tried the one irresistible thing:

I got a supply of small earthworms, and, stalking him, tossed them so as to cause them to fall near him, and he saw and knew what they were, and swallowed them hungrily; and he saw, too, that they were thrown to him by a hand, and that the hand was part of that same huge grey-clad monster that had a little while back so furiously hunted him; and at once he seemed to understand the meaning of it all, and instead of flying from he ran to meet us, and, recovering his voice called to be fed.

In one day he became tame and thereafter required feeding at roughly three hourly intervals, calling at all the doors and windows of the cottage in turn. Hudson continues:

It was most amusing to see him, when, on our return from a long walk or a day out, he would come to meet us, screaming excitedly, bounding over the lawn with long hops, looking like a miniature very dark-coloured kangaroo. One day I came back alone to the cottage, and sat down on the lawn in a canvas chair, to wait for my companion who had the key. The blackbird had seen, and came flying to me, and pitching close to my feet began crying to be fed, shaking his wings, and dancing about in a most excited state, for he had been left a good many hours without food, and was very hungry. As I moved not in my chair he presently ran round and began screaming and fluttering on the other side of it, thinking, I suppose, that he had gone to the wrong place, and that by addressing himself to the back of my head he would quickly get an answer. Up to the very last, when he had grown as hardy and strong on the wing as any of his wild companions, he kept up his acquaintance with and confidence in us; and even at nights when I would go out to where most of our wild birds roosted, in the trees and bushes growing in a vast old chalk pit close to the cottage, and called 'Blackie', instantly there would be a response, a softly chuckled note, like a sleepy 'Good-night', thrown back to me out of the darkness.

W. H. Hudson (1841–1922): 'An Orphaned Blackbird'

The confidence the blackbird shows in man is comparatively recent, as up to the middle of the last century it was a shy, woodland bird. Now, there are very few places in Britain where it has not become established. Perhaps the main reason for its success is an ability to eat a wide variety of foods. Fruit of all kinds, especially pears, apples, cherries, or raspberries it finds irresistible – and this fondness loses the bird a lot of friends.

But then, as Joseph Addison, the founder of *The Spectator* reminded us over 250 years ago: 'I value my garden more for being full of blackbirds than of cherries, and very frankly give them fruit for their songs.'

But it is not only fruit. A Mr Henry Hyslop from Warnborough, Oxfordshire wrote to *The Field* on 6 June 1914: 'Whilst sitting out on my lawn on 29th May, my attention was attracted by a blackbird chasing something in a near-by border. Presently it appeared with a small frog in its bill, which it killed by successive pecks, and on being disturbed it flew away with its prey.'

Unlike his relation the song thrush, the blackbird does not make a speciality of cracking snail shells, although sometimes even here he makes a picking. I have often watched a blackbird dash in to make off with the prize at the precise moment that a thrush finally opens the shell. This is opportunism of a high order.

Early morning or evening is the time to watch him hunting down that important part of his diet, the earthworm. The blackbird knows that dampness brings the worms to the surface and he sets about the job with total concentration. With hops and quick rushes he quarters the lawn; a pause, as he cocks his head for intensive listening. That is how it appears to us but, in fact, he is probably more concerned with looking. This is because his eyes are set at the side of the head and fixed in their sockets so the bird has to angle his head to scan the ground near its feet. A trace of movement in the grass and down shoots that golden bill for a long, hard pull.

A blackbird seen in late summer squatting with wings spread close to the ground and a rapt expression is almost certainly anting.

He may be so engrossed that a close approach is possible. At this time when ants are swarming for their mating flights, the bird is thought to experience a sensuous pleasure by allowing them to run over its plumage. Ants, when aroused, squirt formic acid. This presumably not only stimulates the skin but also acts as an insecticide. Sometimes birds deliberately place crushed ants among the feathers to assist plumage maintenance.

Blackbirds and most garden birds also like to sun themselves, lying with their tails and one or both wings spread. This may also help with feather care, and they certainly appear to enjoy it.

Preening, with special attention to the flight feathers and tail, is vital. The preen gland is just above the tail and contains oil which the bird works into the plumage and skin. The most thorough preen is after bathing when the oil spreads more effectively.

There is no better time to watch a blackbird than when it is taking its pleasure in a shallow bird-bath. First, with feathers fluffed up, it dips forward, violently shaking its bill from side to side, and flicking its wings. It then squats back with its tail in the water flicking its wings upwards and sending water flying in all directions. The two movements alternate but no great time is spent at the bath through fear of predators. Then, the elaborate preening sequence follows.

Sometimes a hen bird is mistaken for a thrush. Her colouring is dark-brown with a pale throat and underparts mottled and spotted. Also she has a brown bill. The juveniles are lighter still and again the underparts are speckled. It is only in the second year that the males get their splendid yellow bill, until then it is blackish.

Blackbirds also have a tendency to be albinos or partial albinos with flecks or patches of white. One theory is that this may be caused by a deficiency in diet. There certainly seem to be more of these birds in suburban gardens than in the countryside and perhaps some of them have become over dependent on bird-tables for their food. Most of us I suspect are well content with the blackbird as he is. A final tribute comes from an anonymous pen of another century:

> In midst of woods or pleasant groves,
> Where all sweet birds do sing,
> Methought I heard so rare a sound
> Which made the heavens to ring.

The Blackbird

The charm was good, the noise full sweet,
Each bird did play his part;
And I admired to hear the same;
Joy sprang into my heart.

The blackbird made the sweetest sound,
Whose tunes did far excel;
Full pleasantly, and most profound
Was all things placed well.

Thy pretty tunes, mine own sweet bird,
Done with so good a grace,
Extol thy name, prefer the same
Abroad in every place.

Thy music grave, bedeckéd well
With sundry points of skill
Bewrays thy knowledge excellent
Ingrafted in thy will.

My tongue shall speak, my pen shall write
In praise of thee to tell;
The sweetest bird that ever was –
In friendly sort farewell!

Anon.

7

The Song Thrush and the Mistle Thrush

> That's the wise thrush; he sings each song twice over,
> Lest you should think he never could recapture
> The first fine careless rapture!
>
> *Robert Browning (1812–1889)*

Compared with the blackbird's mellow, meditative notes, his close relation the song thrush is a treble. Which is the finer songster is arguable, but without doubt the thrush is the principal herald of spring. Sometimes he sings in autumn and winter too, August and September being his only quiet months. The thrush, or to give his old names – the mavis or throstle – unlike the blackbird uses no set phrase in his song. It is almost as though he were improvising and, as Browning noted, frequently repeats a short sequence two or three times.

But, for me, no poet caught more perfectly the spirit of the throstle's song than Alfred, Lord Tennyson. To read his lines is to hear again that age-old promise of better times – ringing out on a still evening at the turn of the year:

> Summer is coming, summer is coming,
> I know it, I know it, I know it.
> Light again, leaf again, life again, love again,
> Yes, my wild little poet.
>
> Sing the new year in under the blue,
> Last year you sang it as gladly.

94

The Song Thrush and the Mistle Thrush

'New, new, new, new!' Is it then *so* new
That you should carol so madly?

'Love again, song again, nest again, young again,'
Never a prophet so crazy!
And hardly a daisy as yet, little friend,
See, there is hardly a daisy.

'Here again, here, here, here, happy year!'
O warble unchidden, unbidden!
Summer is coming, is coming, my dear,
And all the winters are hidden.
Alfred, Lord Tennyson (1809–1892): 'The Throstle'

The thrush, for some reason, has acquired a reputation for wisdom. Perhaps that is why John Keats in one of his barren spells consoled himself by imagining:

What The Thrush Said

O thou whose face hath felt the Winter's wind,
Whose eye has seen the snow-clouds hung in mist,
And the black elm tops 'mong the freezing stars,
To thee the spring will be a harvest-time.
O thou, whose only book has been the light
Of supreme darkness which thou feddest on
Night after night when Phoebus was away,
To thee the spring shall be a triple morn.
O fret not after knowledge – I have none,
And yet my song comes native with the warmth.
O fret not after knowledge – I have none,
And yet the Evening listens. He who saddens
At thought of idleness cannot be idle,
And he's awake who thinks himself asleep.
John Keats (1795–1821)

Sometimes people have difficulty in distinguishing between the song thrush and his close relation the mistle thrush. The mistle thrush is the larger of the two and greyish-brown on the upper parts, while the song thrush is a slightly more reddish-brown.

Another difference is that the former has outer tail feathers tipped with white and its spots are larger and more conspicuous than those of the song thrush. It also has white patches on the undersides of its wings which are seen clearly in flight. There would be less confusion perhaps if the mistle thrush's old name of stormcock was in more general use. No name could be more apt, as it seems to love to rise to an occasion and sing defiance at the weather.

The song is more continuous and less varied than the song thrush's but its shrill tones are full of character and carry clearly in wind and rain. At the Suffolk cottage, where the garden is only about a mile back from the North Sea, we get all the winds that blow. I have often seen the stormcock perched on the topmost bough of a wych elm, tossing in a January gale, and thrilled to hear his clarion call.

That great nineteenth-century nature writer Richard Jefferies when composing one of his meditative essays was once interrupted in like fashion:

While thus thinking, suddenly there rang out three clear, trumpet-like notes from a tree at the edge of the copse by the garden. A softer song followed, and then again the same three notes, whose wild sweetness echoed through the wood.

The voice of the missel-thrush sounded not only close at hand and in the room, but repeated itself as it floated away, as the bugle-call does. He is the trumpeter of spring: Lord of March, his proud call challenges the woods; there are none who can answer. Listen for the missel-thrush: when he sings the snow may fall, the rain drift, but not for long; the violets are near at hand.

Jefferies uses there the old spelling of 'missel'. The name was of course given to the stormcock because of his liking for mistletoe berries.

As Tennyson magically caught the spirit of the song thrush's notes so does Ruth Pitter make one see afresh and thrill to the sound of the stormcock. On entering an old shed one winter's day to look for something, she was surprised by a burst of song close by; glancing up through a gap in the roof – suddenly she saw him in all his glory:

A Celebration of Birds

Scarcely at arm's-length from the eye,
Myself unseen, I saw him there;
The throbbing throat that made the cry,
The breast dewed from the misty air,
The polished bill that opened wide
And showed the pointed tongue inside:

The large eye, ringed with many a ray
Of minion feathers, finely laid,
The feet that grasped the elder-spray:
How strongly used, how subtly made
The scale, the sinew, and the claw,
Plain through the broken roof I saw;

The flight-feathers in tail and wing,
The shorter coverts, and the white
Merged into russet, marrying
The bright breast to the pinions bright,
Gold sequins, spots of chestnut, shower
Of silver, like a brindled flower.

Soldier of fortune, northwest Jack,
Old hard-times' braggart, there you blow!
But tell me ere your bagpipes crack
How you can make so brave a show,
Full-fed in February, and dressed
Like a rich merchant at a feast.

One-half the world, or so they say,
Knows not how half the world may live;
So sing your song and go your way,
And still in February contrive
As bright as Gabriel to smile
On elder-spray by broken tile.

Ruth Pitter (1897–   ): extract from 'Stormcock in Elder'

Another sure way of identifying the mistle thrush is by its flight call – a harsh, grating cry – which can rise to a strident scream when its eggs or young are threatened. In comparison, the alarm rattle of the song thrush is softer and less frequently heard. Thomas Hardy wrote one of the most famous thrush poems and I feel he too must have been listening to the stormcock rather than the song thrush. It would appear small because it was singing at the top of a tree. The bird was certainly challenging the elements in characteristic style, as Hardy leant on a gate that winter's evening with the countryside gripped in frost:

> I leant upon a coppice gate
>   When Frost was spectre-gray,
> And Winter's dregs made desolate
>   The weakening eye of day.
> The tangled bine-stems scored the sky
>   Like strings of broken lyres,
> And all mankind that haunted nigh
>   Had sought their household fires.
>
> The land's sharp features seemed to be
>   The Century's corpse outleant,
> His crypt the cloudy canopy,
>   The wind his death-lament.
> The ancient pulse of germ and birth
>   Was shrunked hard and dry,
> And every spirit upon earth
>   Seemed fervourless as I.
>
> At once a voice arose among
>   The bleak twigs overhead
> In a full-hearted evensong
>   Of joy illimited;
> An aged thrush, frail, gaunt, and small,
>   In blast-beruffled plume,
> Had chosen thus to fling his soul
>   Upon the growing gloom.
>
> So little cause for carrollings
>   Of such ecstatic sound
> Was written on terrestrial things
>   Afar or nigh around,
> That I could think there trembled through
>   His happy good-night air
> Some blessed Hope, whereof he knew
>   And I was unaware.
>   *Thomas Hardy (1840–1928): 'The Darkling Thrush'*

Andrew Young, the Scottish nature poet, also wrote of the missel thrush and he well knew of the bird's liking for the tops of trees:

> That missel-thrush
> Scorns to alight on a low bush,
> And as he flies
> And tree-top after tree-top tries,
> His shadow flits
> And harmlessly on tree-trunk hits.
>
> Shutting his wings
> He sways and sings and sways and sings,
> And from his bough
> As in deep water he looks through
> He sees me there
> Crawl at the bottom of the air.
>
> *Andrew Young (1885–1971): 'The Missel Thrush'*

F. O. Morris in his *A History of British Birds* champions the song thrush in his grandiloquent, nineteenth-century style:

As for the note, that man can have no music in his soul, who does not love the gladsome song of the Throstle. Who would not stand still to listen to it in the tranquil summer evening, and look for the place of the songster?

The calm eventide is the hour at which he most delights to sing, and rich and eloquent then, as always, are his strains. Uninterruptedly, he warbles the full and harmonious sounds, which now rise in strength, and now fall in measured cadence, filling your ear with the ravishing melody, and now die away so soft and low, that they are scarcely audible. If you alarm him, you break the charm; the minstrel will suddenly cease, and silently drop into the underwood beneath.

It must also have been a throstle that made poor Susan so homesick for the green fields and dales of Cumberland in William Wordsworth's sad little poem. This was a caged bird that she used to hear singing in the heart of the City:

The Reverie of Poor Susan

> At the corner of Wood Street, when daylight appears,
> Hangs a Thrush that sings loud, it has sung for three years:

Poor Susan has pass'd by the spot, and has heard
In the silence of morning the song of the bird.

'Tis a note of enchantment: what ails her? She sees
A mountain ascending, a vision of trees;
Bright volumes of vapour through Lothbury glide,
And a river flows on through the vale of Cheapside.

Green pastures she views in the midst of the dale,
Down which she so often has tripp'd with her pail;
And a single small cottage, a nest like a dove's,
The one only dwelling on earth that she loves.

She looks, and her heart is in heaven: but they fade,
The mist and the river, the hill and the shade;
The stream will not flow, and the hill will not rise,
And the colours have all pass'd away from her eyes!

Up to the end of the nineteenth century when it was happily made illegal to put British songbirds in cages, many a thrush must have sung his heart out from the confines of a tiny prison. As late as 1885 the ornithologist W. T. Greene was writing: 'With common care a Thrush will live in a cage for fifteen or twenty years, but its domicile must be roomy, and the utmost attention to cleanliness is indispensable in order to prevent its feathers from being broken and spoiled.'

Far from cities and cages is W. Macgillivray's thrush, serenading its loved one in glorious freedom and, characteristically, a note or short phrase is repeated in case it might have been missed the first time:

The Thrush's Song

Dear, dear, dear,
   Is the rocky glen,
Far away, far away, far away
   The haunts of men.

Here shall we dwell in love
With the lark and the dove,
Cuckoo and cornrail;
Feast on the banded snail,
   Worm and gilded fly;

Drink of the crystal rill
Winding adown the hill,
  Never to dry.

With glee, with glee, with glee,
  Cheer up, cheer up, cheer up, here
Nothing to harm us, then sing merrily,
  Sing to the loved one whose nest is near.

Qui, qui, qui, queeu, quip,
Tiurru, tiurru, chipiwi,
Too-tee, too-tee, chiu-choo,
Chirri, chirri, chooee,
Quiu, qui, qui!

The song thrush makes her nest with great care and artistry using mud as a lining. What a marvel it is that in her very first nesting season, without practice or example, the young bird is able to fashion a piece of work with such meticulous craftsmanship:

Watch how the hen Thrush brings beakfuls of mud, small pieces of rotten wood, and cow or horse-dung and kneads them up together in the bottom of her nest and then plasters them evenly around the inside, working upwards until the whole is covered to within half an inch of the rim, and how she then weaves the grass, or moss, over and into the upper edge of mud and finally, using her breast as a smoothing agent, renders the whole of the inside perfectly circular by rotating first one way and then the other, even going to the trouble of wetting her breast feathers in a nearby pond so as to ensure that the mud shall not dry out and lose cohesion before the smoothing is completed. The result is as true as if it had been turned on a potter's wheel.

    C. Percival Staples: 'Birds in a Garden Sanctuary'

The song thrush can have had no more devoted observer than John Clare, who liked nothing better than to conceal himself in the hedgerow at nesting time:

The Thrush's Nest

Within a thick and spreading hawthorn bush,
That overhung a molehill large and round,

The Song Thrush and the Mistle Thrush

I heard from morn to morn a merry thrush
Sing hymns to sunrise, and I drank the sound
With joy; and often, an intruding guest,
I watched her secret toil from day to day, –
How she warped the moss, to form a nest,
And modelled it within with wood and clay;
And by and by, like heath-bells gilt with dew,
There lay her shining eggs, as bright as flowers,
Ink-spotted-over shells of greeny blue;
And there I witnessed, in the sunny hours
A brood of Nature's minstrels chirp and fly
Glad as the sunshine and the laughing sky.

How vivid still is the childhood memory of being lifted up beside the hedgerow; and then the first shy peep inside the nest at those wondrous eggs. The usual number is five and there may be two or three broods from March to July. The most favoured sites are fairly low down in a bush or hedge, although, like the blackbird's nest it might be almost anywhere. A correspondent wrote to *Animal World* on the 1 May 1871 with a somewhat extreme case:

At a slate quarry belonging to a friend of mine, a thrush thought proper to build her nest on a ridge in the very centre of which they were constantly blasting the rock. At first she was much discomposed by the fragments flying in all directions, but still she would not quit her chosen locality. She soon observed that a bell rang whenever a train was about to be fired, and that at the notice, the workmen retired to a safe position. In a few days, when she heard the bell, she quitted her exposed situation and flew down to where the workmen sheltered themselves, dropping close to their feet. There she would remain until the explosion had taken place, and then return to her nest.

The working men observing this narrated it to their employers, and it was also told to visitors who came to the quarry. The visitors naturally expressed a wish to witness so curious a specimen of intellect, but as the rock could not always be ready to be blasted when visitors came, the bell was rung instead, and, for a few times, answered the purpose. The thrush flew down as usual close to where they stood but she soon perceived that she was trifled with, the explosion not following. The consequence was, afterwards, when the bell was rung, she would peep over the ledge to ascertain if the workmen did retreat, and if they did not, she would quietly retain her position, probably saying to herself, 'No, no, gentlemen, I'm not to be roused off my eggs, just for your amusement.'

A distinctly canny bird.

The usual time for incubation is fourteen days, followed by another fortnight, after which the fledglings are ready to leave the nest. From a hide, Alec Robertson kept a watch on two nests in laurel bushes, a few yards apart, and described the young thrushes leap into the unknown:

With much backsliding and flapping of wings one of them ascended a branch until it was about two feet above the nest. There it remained, round-eyed with the novelty of its experiences, until a gust of wind caused it to overbalance and it fell straight back into the nest. The next adventurer was not so fortunate, for he fell to the ground, and the presence of a roving cat caused absolute pandemonium among both pairs of thrushes and the two pairs of blackbirds which were nesting close by. He hopped gamely along however, and I lost sight of him, but by some remarkable freak of providence he finished up by ascending into the second thrush's nest and relaxing in great comfort on top of the much smaller young.

A. W. P. Robertson: 'Birds Wild and Free'

It is not without reason that a thrush will often build its nest in a bush of close-cut thorn. This can be a sure defence against any large predator. On 17 April 1936 A. W. Boyd wrote:

In a quickset hedge outside my window is a song-thrush's nest within a few yards of the house. One morning as I glanced outside I was aware of something lying flat against the hedge, and suddenly realised that I was looking at a hen sparrow-hawk, which with wings and tail widespread was balancing itself there in an attempt to get at the throstle inside the close-cut thorns. It flew off, hard-faced but unsatisfied, and later in the day I was delighted to see the thrush sitting placidly on its eggs as if nothing had ever happened to frighten it.

A. W. Boyd: from 'The Country Diary of a Cheshire Man'

The mistle thrush is the earlier breeder, sometimes even before the end of February, and often chooses the fork of a tall tree for its large, untidy nest, although there is much variation of the site. At that time of year cover is scarce and the nest is highly vulnerable to raids – especially from the crow family. Not surprisingly the birds are very wary and one of the pair usually remains on guard near the nest. The mistle thrush is valiant in defence of its eggs or young and is one of the few birds that will, if necessary, attack a human intruder. Gilbert White noted its courage in a letter to the Honourable Daines Barrington on 13 September 1774:

The missel-thrush is, while breeding, fierce and pugnacious, driving such birds as approach its nest, with great fury, to a distance. The Welch call it 'pen y llwyn', the head or master of the coppice. He suffers no magpie, jay or blackbird, to enter the garden where he haunts; and is, for the time, a good guard to the new-sown legumens. In general he is very successful in defence of his family: but once I observed in my garden, that several magpies came determined to storm the nest of a missel-thrush: the dams defended their mansion with great vigour, and fought resolutely 'pro aris & focis'; but numbers at last prevailed, they tore the nest to pieces, and swallowed the young alive.

No wonder the bird is so much on its guard!

When nesting in orchards the cover offered to it by mistletoe must be most welcome. On 1 September 1900 a Mr George Calcott was prompted to write to *Country Life*:

In a most interesting article on 'Yorkshire Bird Life' which appears in your issue of August 11th, Mr. Graham says that he has rarely seen a missel-thrush's nest actually situated in a clump of mistletoe. It may, therefore, interest him to know that in an orchard adjoining this garden (Olveston, Glos.) it is the exception to find a nest which is not built in or very close to mistletoe. There is an exceptionally large quantity of mistletoe growing in this orchard, and the extra cover it gives to the nest is doubtless the reason of the birds preferring it as a site ...

Mistle thrushes are not birds that often visit suburban gardens and are more likely to be seen, after the breeding season, when they move about over open country in family flocks. There are usually two broods and the young of the first often join those of the second to make up quite large parties foraging for berries of mistletoe, mountain ash, yew and so on. Although the sexes are much alike, the young are yellower on the upper parts and the head, back and wings are spotted with white.

The song thrush eats more earthworms and insects than his larger relation and to watch a pair of them quartering the lawn after rain is to feel a certain sympathy for the worms. Ted Hughes, the least sentimental of contemporary poets, finds them quite frightening:

> Terrifying are the attent sleek thrushes on the lawn,
> More coiled steel than living – a poised
> Dark deadly eye, those delicate legs
> Triggered to stirrings beyond sense – with a start, a bounce, a stab
> Overtake the instant and drag out some writhing thing.
> No indolent procrastinations and no yawning stares,
> No sighs or head-scratchings. Nothing but bounce and stab
> And a ravening second.
> *Ted Hughes (1930–   ): extract from 'Thrushes' from 'Lupercal'*

Evidently a thrush will occasionally welcome a change of diet as A. E. Armstrong witnessed: 'The most extraordinary aberration of feeding-habit I ever witnessed, however, was the behaviour of a Song-Thrush I watched at Oxford some years ago, as it was running along the edge of the stream that flows through Magdalen College grounds; suddenly it dashed into the water and secured one of a shoal of minnows, which it beat on the ground and then swallowed whole.'

Both thrushes eat snails, although the song thrush is the greater addict of the two. We must all at some time have watched one busy at his anvil on a day in high summer:

He searches about under the ivy, under which the snails hide in their shells in the heat of the day, and brings them forth into the light. The shell is too large for his beak to hold it pincer-fashion, but at the entrance – the snail's doorway – he can thrust his bill in, and woe then to the miserable occupant! With a hop and flutter the thrush mounts the stone anvil, and there destroys his victim in workmanlike style. Up goes his head, lifting the snail high in the air, and then, smash! the shell comes down on the stone with all the force he can use. About two such blows break the shell, and he then coolly chips the fragments off as you might from an egg, and makes very few mouthfuls of the contents. On the stone and round about it lie the fragments of many such shells – relics of former feasts.

Richard Jefferies (1848–1887): 'Wildlife in a Southern County'

The Song Thrush and the Mistle Thrush

In the Outer Hebrides the thrushes are darker in colour and they have a great liking for whelks, in spite of the hardness of their shells. A naturalist, D. M., wrote on 23 December 1926:

The song-thrush of Mull has one habit which I have not noted in birds of the species elsewhere, for in winter it lives by carrying whelks from the seaweed-covered rocks to a suitably sized and shaped stone, where it breaks the shells, an effort during which the bird has to exert its full strength. The human operator who wishes to break the shell of a whelk invariably tries to do so by hammering it on its hard upper side with a stone, but the thrush is not so foolish, so it holds the whelk in its beak in such a manner as to allow of its bringing the soft under-shell in contact with the stone it uses as an anvil. Any 'anvil' is not good enough for the thrush's purpose, and it searches until it finds one of just the right size and shape, when, as seen by the scattered shells, it breaks up its whole food supply.

This whelk-eating by the thrushes of Mull is most evidently not a matter of taste but of necessity, for when the frost and snow are gone the birds return quickly to their everyday diet of snails and worms. It is notable that when frost is in prospect the birds become very hungry in advance of the actual hardening of the ground, and this is probably because the worms, slugs, snails, etc., are extremely sensitive to cold and dive deeply into the earth at any sudden fall of temperature.

Eric Parker: extract from 'Oddities of Natural History'

Extremes of weather do not suit the thrushes. The terrible winters of 1947 and 1963 took a heavy toll, as did the prolonged drought of 1976. They do not seem to have the toughness and adaptability of their cousin the blackbird. There are few sadder sights than an emaciated song thrush, searching endlessly for worms, over sun-baked earth. Let us hope he will maintain his numbers; spring would be bereft without its speckled singer:

> Bid him come, for on his wings
> The sunny year he bringeth,
> And the heart unlocks its springs
> Wheresoe'er he singeth.

Cornwall 1787–1874

8

The Starling

Starlings are among the chief go-getters of the bird world: watch them feeding – they are forever racing over the ground, pushing and bustling, lest another of their kind should outsmart them. Frequently they will leave a whole tract of field or lawn untouched, so determined is each one of them to be first at the next feeding place.

In appearance too, the starling is something of a city-slicker, flashy, in his dark plumage and with a sharp, knowing look. He is even a commuter; but in reverse. On late summer evenings, when the homeward bound crowds press wearily through city streets, few among them even bother to glance up at the great formations of starlings manoeuvring overhead. Yet the air is filled with a shrill screaming as flock after flock of birds pour in from the countryside to their chosen roosting places, where they stand, jostling, shoulder to shoulder, high up on window-ledges, cornices, and roofs.

In London, the National Gallery, St Martin-in-the-Fields and other buildings around Trafalgar Square are much favoured.

> An image up there like an early film
> Flickering through a modern projector,
> The starlings circle above the spires,
> And the flock is a heart beating.
>
> It is not our heart, we who below
> Greet them and hear the foreign chatter –
> The starlings inhabit a region of ceilings,
> While we on the floors of city ravines
> Watch them arriving from the sky

The Starling

With wonder that lintels of office windows,
Balustrades, friezes, plinths, corbels
Should be welcome to them as mountain rock.
    Clifford Dyment (1914–   ): 'Starlings in Trafalgar Square'

Starlings are less dependent on man for food than is the sparrow, and they will fly up to thirty miles daily along well-defined flight lines to fields and open places, where they forage for insects and grubs. On the other hand, when in need, they can eat almost anything – seeds, fruit or scraps. They only took to roosting in cities at about the turn of the century; in the country, they have always chosen woods, reed-beds, rhododendron thickets or, sometimes, shrubberies of laurel. Viscount Grey, British Foreign Secretary from 1905 to 1916, described a mass roost at his home Fallodon, Northumberland, in the twenties:

The evening flight of starlings over their chosen roosting-place in autumn and winter is one of the marvels of flying. The birds assemble, small parties coming to the chosen spot from any direction after the business of the day is over. They then fly at speed above the roosting-place: a vast globe, it may be, of some thousands of birds. They fly close together, and there are many evolutions and swift turns, yet there is no collision: the impulse to each quick movement or change of direction seems to seize every bird simultaneously. It is as if for the time being each bird had ceased to be a separate entity and had become a part of one sentient whole: one great body, the movement of whose parts was co-ordinated by one impulse or one will affecting them all at the same moment. For some time this wonderful performance continues, then as the globe passes over the laurels a little avalanche of starlings descends, making a rushing noise as it penetrates the stiff leaves. Party after party of starlings now detaches itself and descends each time that the globe passes over the spot, till at length there is but one small party left flying, and this, too, presently descends. There are now hundreds, or it may be thousands, of birds in the evergreens, and for a while there is fuss and chatter; so loud is the noise that I have known it mistaken at a little distance for the sound of a waterfall.
    Viscount Grey of Fallodon (1862–1933): 'The Charm of Birds'

Alec Robertson particularly noticed the heat and smell from a roost:

In November 1953, a friend complained of a large roost in a wood of two acres; four of us, all with previous experience of estimating bird-flocks, watched them come in for an hour before sunset, and recorded a total of 300,000 at a conservative minimum. So closely did they pack on the low trees that one could feel the heat radiating from them at a distance of ten yards, and their musty smell was nauseating.

A. W. P. Robertson: 'Bird Pageant'

Perhaps it is no wonder that these roosts are not regarded with unalloyed joy especially in the cities. Innumerable methods have been used to try to dissuade them from settling on buildings. The Ministry of the Environment have experimented with stuffed owls, fireworks and bird distress calls. The only effective deterrent seems to have been a strip of plastic gel laid along the roosting ledges. This makes it difficult for the birds to get a grip; but it is expensive to fix.

In the country the effect of the roosts can be an even more serious matter. At one time in the 1950's, all the starlings of east Cornwall for some reason considered that a Sitka spruce plantation on Bodmin Moor would make the ideal place to pass the night. One particular area of twenty acres was chosen. From October until March, upwards of a million starlings congregated nightly in a mammoth roost. In an extreme case like this, the concentration of droppings soon poisons the soil. It takes anything from six months to two years for the trees to die, and then the starlings move on to another part of the forest. Conifer plantations, set among wide stretches of grazing land, are particularly vulnerable, as the birds are apt to make a dead-set at them.

A huge flock can be dangerous too. The naturalist Richard Kearton wrote in the twenties of how the birds had even put on the brakes of a train: 'A flock of starlings recently collided with a Welsh railway engine. The impact was powerful enough to apply the vacuum brakes and bring the whole train to a standstill. The unique character of an accident of this kind can only be fully realised by anyone familiar with the wonderful wing power and acute mentality of members of this species.'

In our day, airfields must be kept clear of big flocks in case they get sucked into the jets.

The ornithologist and writer W. K. Richmond had an odd experience with starlings one night on the Norfolk Broads in the 1930's.

I notice he uses the old English word 'chirm' meaning the mingled voices of many birds:

It was night-time late in October when I made my first acquaintance with Hickling, and rowed through inscrutable darkness across the black, oily waters. Here and there a pale spectre of a Mute Swan appeared, and went surging past, snorting to itself, to disappear in ghostly fashion into the dark. Somewhere ahead was a confused, loud murmur of sound, very mysterious if not to say awe inspiring. It consisted of a vague chirm as if from a million suppressed voices which now and then rose suddenly to a passionate intensity, and a noise of falling water like the roar of a cascade heard in the distance. Sometimes the two blended noises would drop off into a complete silence quite suddenly, and then grow up again to their former intensity. It is easy to smile in broad daylight at the pale relation in black and white of such an experience, but to me for a few minutes it seemed as if some power were abroad that night, as if great mysterous spirits were moving about on the face of the dark waters, perhaps those

> Presences of Nature in the sky
> And on the earth! Ye visions of the hills!
> And Souls of lonely places!

of which Wordsworth speaks in *The Prelude*.

At length, of course, a more prosaic explanation presented itself. On nearer approach the first noise became recognizable as that of an immense army of starlings which had encamped for the night in one of the reed beds and which were evidently solacing themselves by a little hushed community singing. Londoners who have seen these birds huddled in hundreds on the ledge of the National Gallery and in nooks and corners of St. Martin-in-the-Fields, will have remarked their singing which sounds shrilly late at night above the roaring and grinding of the traffic. In the present instance, coming across the waters in the stillness of the night, the sound was most moving.

W. K. Richmond: 'England's Birds'

In the autumn of 1975 with the BBC 'Nationwide' cameras I visited one of Britain's most famous roosts on and around Bristol's Templemeads Station. The building is a splendid example of Victorian Gothic, as befits that great railway engineer Brunel, and the starlings have certainly given it the mark of their approval. At dusk small parties began moving in and soon there were great clouds of them dividing and coming together again with the harmony of a well-disciplined army. The BBC's Jeffery Boswall, who is an authority on the starling, said he thought the roosts probably served as information centres. It certainly seems possible that, apart from warmth and security, the birds may find them useful places in which to pool knowledge of the best available feeding grounds.

Whether in town or country there is no sure-fire way of moving the starlings on, once they have gathered. They do not arrive until dusk and then, as soon as it gets dark, they feel secure and will not budge. Shooting them is not the answer, as that great bird-lover W. H. Hudson was delighted to witness in the village of Abbotsbury in 1909:

I am always delighted to come on one of these places where starlings congregate, to watch them coming in at day's decline and listen to their marvellous hubbub, and finally to see their aerial evolutions when they rise and break up in great bodies and play at clouds in the sky. When the people of the place, the squire and keepers and others who have an interest in the reeds and osiers, fall to abusing them on account of the damage they do, I put my fingers in my ears. But at Abbotsbury I did not do so, but listened with keen pleasure to the curses they evented and the story they told. This was that when the owner of Abbotsbury came down for the October shooting and found the starlings more numerous than ever, he put himself into a fine passion and reproached his keepers and other servants for not having got rid of the birds as he had desired them to do. Some of them ventured to say that it was easier said than done, whereupon the great man swore that he would do it himself without assistance from anyone, and getting out a big duck-gun he proceeded to load it with the smallest shot and went down to the reed bed and concealed himself among the bushes at a suitable distance. The birds were pouring in, and when it was growing dark and they had settled down for the night he fired his big piece into the thick of the crowd, and by-and-by when the birds after wheeling about for a minute or two settled down again in the same place he fired again. Then he went home, and early next morning men and boys went into the reeds and gathered a bushel or so of dead starlings. But the birds returned in their thousands that evening, and his heart being still hot against them he went out a second time to slaughter them wholesale with his big gun. Then when he had blazed into the crowd once more, and the dead and wounded fell like rain into the water below, the revulsion came

and he was mad with himself for having done such a thing, and on his return to the house, or palace, he angrily told his people to 'let the starlings alone' for the future – never to molest them again!
W. H. Hudson (1841–1922): 'Abbotsbury Starlings' from 'Afoot in England'

The Abbotsbury landowner might also have considered the good the birds do at other seasons of the year. When nesting and feeding its young, each pair is spread out over the land and consuming insect life of all kinds at a tremendous rate. This probably more than offsets the damage done at the roosts.

> Tonight this sunset spreads two golden wings
> Cleaving the western sky;
> Wing'd too with wind it is, and winnowings
> Of birds; as if the day's last hour in rings
> Of strenuous flight must die.
>
> Sun-steeped in fire, the homeward pinions sway
> Above the dovecote-tops;
> And clouds of starlings 'ere they rest with day,
> Sink clamorous like mill-waters at wild play,
> By turns in every copse.
>
> Each tree heart-deep the wrangling rout receives,
> Save for the whirr within,
> You could not tell the starlings from the leaves;
> Then one great puff of wings, and the swarm heaves
> Away with all its din.
>   *D. G. Rossetti (1828–1882): 'Sunset Wings'*

Sometimes I am asked how it is that a bird does not drop off a branch when it falls asleep? The answer is that when the bird perches, tendons passing down the back of the legs automatically tighten so that the toes curl in. Three toes, of course, point forwards and one backwards; it is the middle toe in particular that locks firmly on to the branch. Then, as soon as the bird stands erect again, the tension on the tendons is released, and the bird can move freely.

Many writers have been fascinated by starling roosts, but not so many by its song. And yet:

The Starling

Of all the birds whose tuneful throats
Do welcome in the verdant spring,
I prefer the steerling's notes,
And think she does most sweetly sing.
Allan Ramsay (1686–1758): 'A Song' from 'The Poets' Birds'

So wrote Allan Ramsay over 200 years ago. And there was no greater admirer of the starling's vocal powers than Hudson who took especial delight in such curiously contrasted sounds:

The airy whistle, the various chirp, the clink-clink as of a cracked bell, the low chatter of mixed harsh and musical sounds, the kissing and finger-cracking, and those long metallic notes, as of a saw being filed not un-musically, or (as a friend suggests) as of milking a cow in a tin pail; how-ever familiar you may be with the starling, you cannot listen to one of their choirs without hearing some new sound. There is more variety in the starling than in any other species, and not only in his language; if you observe him closely for a short time, he will treat you to a sudden and surprising transformation. Watch him when absorbed in his own music, especially when emitting his favourite saw-filing or milking-a-cow-in-a-tin-pail sounds: he trembles on his perch – shivers as with cold – his feathers puffed out, his wings hanging as if broken, his beak wide open, and the long pointed feathers of his swollen throat projected like a ragged beard. He is then a most forlorn-looking object, apparently broken up and falling to pieces; suddenly the sounds cease, and in the twinkling of an eye he is once more transformed into the neat, compact, glossy, alert starling!
W. H. Hudson (1841–1922): 'Birds in London'

Another acute observer, Richard Jefferies, was convinced that the starling is often speaking directly to his fellows when he sings. I wonder if this is how information is exchanged among the birds?

A starling is on the chimney-top; yonder on the ash tree are four or five of his acquaintance. Suddenly he begins to pour forth a flood of eloquence – facing them as he speaks: will they come with him down to the field where the cows are grazing? There will be sure to be plenty of insects settling on the grass round the cows, and every now and then they tear up the herbage by the roots and expose creeping things. 'Come' you may hear him say, modulating his tones to persuasion, 'Come quickly; you see it is a fresh piece of grass into which the cows have been turned only a few hours since; it was too long for us before, but where they have eaten we can get at the ground comfortably.

After more cajoling Jefferies' starling explodes:

Will you or will you not? (A sharp, short whistle of interrogation.) You are simply idiots (finishing with a scream of abuse).
I'm off!

> *Richard Jefferies (1848–1887): 'Wild Life in a Southern County'*

And no doubt, his fellows would be after him at once, just in case they might be missing something.

For such a highly sociable bird as the starling his nesting arrangements are surprisingly private. The chosen site is nearly always a hole, but it might be almost anywhere: under the eaves, in a chimney, a pile of stones, a cliff-face or an old tree. He is not above moving in on a woodpecker – uninvited. The green woodpecker or yaffle, although larger and with a much more powerful beak, seems often to be outwitted and evicted.

G. K. Yeates was witness at a break-in:

A yaffle had bored a nesting hole high up in an oak and on this a pair of starlings had their eye. The pecker was in the hole, popping its head in and out in its consternation and indecision at the chattering presence of its tormentors. These were deployed for the attack, one on a branch above the nest, and the other below, and they kept up a continuous stream of verbal abuse. The pecker at last emerged instead of defending its castle from within. One of the starlings nipped into the hole in a trice, while the other scolded and mobbed the rightful owner. When the second woodpecker arrived, it tried to get into the hole. It was a most pitiful sight. It clung to the entrance and popped its head in and out for several minutes, wearing a look of pained surprise at the unfamiliar tenant within. I never saw the starling inside rush to the entrance to frighten away the pecker. It stayed put, clearly believing that possession was nine-tenths of the law. The second starling now harried the second woodpecker and chased it away from the nest. It then stood on guard, and broke up in infancy any attempt at counter-attack by the two yaffles which were climbing disconsolately about the tree. After an hour they flew off, and I doubt not they never returned, for the starlings were in undisputed possession next time I passed.

> *G. K. Yeates: 'Bird Haunts in Southern England'*

The Starling

That great nature poet, who was killed in the First World War, Edward Thomas, in his poem about a decrepit old barn mentions the starlings, who of course like nothing better than a thatched roof to nest in:

Starlings used to sit there with bubbling throats
Making a spiky beard as they chattered
And whistled and kissed, with heads in air,
Till they thought of something else that mattered.

But now they cannot find a place,
Among all those holes, for a nest any more.
It's the turn of lesser things, I suppose.
Once I fancied 'twas starlings they built it for.
'The Barn' from Edward Thomas on the Countryside,
'A Selection of his Prose and Verse'

Perhaps the most remarkable thing of all about the starling is his astonishing gift of mimicry. I remember visiting a farm in Cumbria in the summer of 1975. It was the assembly point for a BBC 'Nationwide' camera team and our object was to film the great colonies of seabirds on the flower-strewn, red sandstone cliff-top of St Bees Head. As we stood in the farmyard discussing our plans, we heard the unmistakable cry of a curlew. The clarity and perfection of the sound made us all look up. There was no curlew to be seen; just one bedraggled starling perched on a broken piece of guttering. He obligingly produced the sound for us again and then flew off with a chuckle, evidently well pleased with the effect he had created.

It's difficult not to believe that the starling has a well-developed sense of humour. Mary Webb's poem is highly fanciful but I, for one, would love to think that this is how young starlings really do behave:

Starlings

When the blue summer night
Is short and safe and light,
How should the starlings any more remember
The fearful, trembling times of dark December?

117

They mimic in their glee,
With impudent jocosity,
The terrible ululation of the owls
That prey
On just such folk as they.
'Tu-whoo!' And rusty-feathered fledglings, pressed
Close in the nest
Amid the chimney-stacks, are good all day
If their indulgent father will but play
At owls,
With predatory howls
And hoots and shrieks and whistlings wild and dread.
Says one small bird
With lids drawn up, cosily tucked in bed,
'Such things were never heard
By me or you.
They are not true'.

This vocal accomplishment of the starling has not always been to its advantage. In less enlightened times, it was often the reason for his ending in a cage. No less a person than Samuel Pepys, when Secretary to the Admiralty, enthused about a talking bird, presumably a mynah, brought from the East Indies by Dr James Pierce, the Duke of York's surgeon. He tells us it was 'black for the greatest part, with the finest collar of white about the neck', talked 'many things', neighed like a horse, and was the best almost that he ever 'heard bird' in his life.

Four years later, Pepys was 'mighty proud' of the talking starling which he acquired through the good offices of Mrs. Martin, the wife of his vain and foolish subordinate, Martin the purser. Mrs. Martin was indebted to the Secretary of the Navy for various little acts of kindness, including the gift of six bottles of claret: when she saw how much he was charmed by the bird she offered to give it to him: nay, better still, she sent her husband round to deliver the gift in person the very next day. The starling had belonged to the King who kept it for a time in his bedchamber. Why he should have parted from it is not explained. Perhaps it whistled too constantly, or spoke out of its turn.

D. M. Stuart: '*A Book of Birds and Beasts*'

In the last century, W. T. Greene, in *Birds I have Kept* quotes an

authority named Bechstein who liked nothing better than popping
a starling into a cage:

This bird becomes wonderfully familiar in the house; as docile and cun-
ning as a dog, he is always gay, wakeful, soon knows all the inhabitants of
the house, remarks their motions and air, and adapts himself to their
humours. In his solemn tottering step, he appears to go stupidly forward;
but nothing escapes his eye. He learns to pronounce words without having
his tongue cut, which proves the uselessness of this cruel operation. He
repeats correctly the airs which are taught him, as does also the female,
imitates the cries of men and animals, and the songs of all the birds in the
room with him. Not only are the young susceptible of these instructions,
the oldest even show the most astonishing docility.

  The Starling is a very hardy bird, and will live for a number of years in
the house. It should, however, be always provided in its cage with a sod of
grass to dig in: and if a few worms are hidden underneath it, the bird will
derive much benefit and enjoyment from its attempts to root them out of
their concealment. Without this precaution the beak of all the starlings,
foreign as well as British, is apt to become long and deformed. The
bottom of the cage must be covered with a thick layer of coarse sand in
order to keep the claws of the feet from getting too long.

  Poor starling. At least he wasn't eaten; but that was only because
he didn't taste very nice. Francis Willoughby, the seventeenth-
century ornithologist who used the old name for the bird and used
capital letters when he felt like it wrote: 'Stares are not eaten in
England by reason of the bitterness of their flesh: The Italians, and
other Outlandish people are not so squeamish, but they can away
with them, and make a dish of them for all that.'

  Surely the most macabre tale of a caged starling comes in
Laurence Sterne's *A Sentimental Journey*. In 1765 Sterne visited Paris
while on a tour of France. While philosophising about the Bastille,
he was disturbed by a voice:

I was interrupted in the hey-day of this soliloquy, with a voice which I took
to be of a child, which complained 'it could not get out'. – I looked up and
down the passage, and seeing neither man, woman, or child, I went out
without further attention.

  In my return back through the passage, I heard the same words repeated twice over; and looking up, I saw it was a starling hung in a little
cage – 'I can't get out – I can't get out', said the starling.

I stood looking at the bird; and to every person who came through the passage, it ran fluttering to the side towards which they approached it, with the same lamentation of its captivity – 'I can't get out', said the starling. God help thee! said I, but I will let thee out, cost what it will; so I turned about the cage to get to the door; it was twisted and double twisted so fast with wire, there was no getting it open without pulling the cage to pieces – I took both hands to it.

The bird flew to the place where I was attempting his deliverance, and thrusting his head through the trellis, pressed his breast against it, as if impatient – I fear poor creature! said I, I cannot set thee at liberty – 'No', said the starling – 'I can't get out – I can't get out', said the starling.

We may be haunted by the thought of that wretched individual bird; but there is no doubt that starlings as a species have been able to spread their wings across the world over the past hundred years or so.

In 1862 settlers introduced them to both islands of New Zealand. Nearly forty years later, a letter from a correspondent in Christchurch who signed himself A.G.H., appeared in *The Spectator*, 19 July 1901:

It may interest you to hear that the starling keeps its reputation here as a 'mocking bird', and like a good colonist adapts itself to altered circumstances. A few days ago I heard one imitate perfectly the cry of the weka (Ocydromus). As these birds are no longer found within miles of Christchurch, it was a puzzle to think where the bird had heard it, until I learnt that an acquaintance a few streets away had recently got one as a pet.

At up-country homesteads I have often heard starlings bleat like young lambs, and my son-in-law tells me he was thoroughly deceived by a starling whose sotto voce bark so exactly resembled that of a dog far away that he twice climbed to the top of a hill, under the impression that the young collie he was training was 'rounding up' sheep on his own account.

The starling empire expanded yet again with their introduction to Australia in 1863, thirty-six birds being set free there. Ever adaptable, they established themselves so successfully that now starlings have spread over half that great continent including the island of Tasmania.

But it was in North America that they found the most suitable conditions of all. In 1890 some joker was seized with the idea that all the birds mentioned in Shakespeare's works should be allowed to live in New York's Central Park. This cosy thought has now produced something like five hundred million starlings from coast to coast.

As they rapidly spread westward it was lamented that the starlings were 'quarrelsome and domineering and are driving our songbirds from the cities'. An American journalist Leonard Dubkin writing in 1947 was philosophical about their success:

If the starling is driving our song-birds from the cities, I say more power to him. Let the song-birds fight for their rights as other creatures do and not sit back and expect to be protected because their song is pleasing to human ears.

Later, he says he thinks it possible that songbirds left the cities of America because of the starlings' horrible appearance:

As a species I think they are the ugliest birds I have ever seen, with their sooty-black plumage, long yellow beaks, and stumpy tails. Seeing a starling on a telephone wire you wonder how he can balance himself, for he has almost no tail at all, and he looks as unsteady as a man doing a handstand on a horizontal bar. His song is the ungodliest noise that ever issued from a living thing, it is a weird hodge-podge of mechanical sounds uttered in a high piercing tone, and reminds me of nothing so much as the sounds that come from a motor-car clutch that needs oiling badly.

Then Dubkin recounts a strange experience he had with a starling in a little park along the lake shore at Chicago Avenue:

One day in the early spring, when the buds were just beginning to open on the trees, I walked into this park to spend an hour or so sitting on the grass, watching the starlings. As soon as the birds saw me they flew to the trees, but I stood quietly a few moments, waiting for them to return to the ground. Most of the flock of about thirty starlings had flown to the highest branches of a tall tree, but one had alighted on the lowest branch of a small tree about fifteen feet from where I stood, and he eyed me curiously from his perch, his long neck stretched forward like a hunting dog, his little stumpy tail jerking convulsively. I had never been very close to a starling before, so I decided to see how intimate I could become with this bird before he flew away. Very slowly and cautiously I moved towards him, expecting him to fly away in alarm at each step I took. But he held his ground until I was almost directly under him, cocking his head from side to side and looking at me first with one eye and then with the other. There we stood for a long time, staring at each other, for I dared not move for fear of frightening him away. Then, very slowly, I began to raise my arm towards him, to see how close he would let my hand come. He continued to move his head from side to side, and though I was sure he could see my hand coming towards him, it was at me that he looked, at my eyes.

Dubkin remembered how snakes are supposed to hypnotise birds and continues:

My hand began to close round his body, but still he did not move. My fingers pinned his wings to his sides, and now he could not have flown away even if he had wanted to. Was there something the matter with him, was he suffering some illness, or had he been hurt? I knew he could fly because I had seen him fly to the tree as I entered the park. I held him in my hand and stared at him wondering what to do next, and he stared up at me. I opened my hand and he lay quietly on his side one eye regarding me. Then, to my surprise and amazement, he scrambled to his feet so that he was standing like an opera singer with his legs spread apart on my palm, stretched his neck up towards my face, opened his beak wide, and began to sing.

Dubkin, a hardboiled newspaperman, began to wonder whether he was dreaming. He went on:

Suddenly the song ended and the bird stood up looking at me with what seemed to me at the time a sort of boastful pride, its head cocked to one side, legs still apart. Then, as though to add the finishing touch to my debasement, it flapped its wings in my face and flew away, off towards the big trees where its fellows were.

Dubkin says he walked away from the park in a daze:

For a long time I could still hear the shrillness of the starling's song in my ears and feel its legs widespread on the palm of my hand; even today these sensations are fresh in my mind, and I suppose I shall carry them with me as long as I live.

The Starling

Dubkin was sensible enough not to try to explain the incident but to set it apart in his memory – a sort of special case.

> After the starlings had flown
> Over the plain and were gone,
> There was one of them stayed on alone
> In the trees; it chattered on high
> Lifting its bill to the sky . . .
> And after a hush
> It gurgled as gurgles a well,
> Warbled as warbles a thrush,
> Had a try at the sound of a bell
> And mimicked a jay . . .
>
> *Ford Madox Hueffer (1873–1939)*

Perhaps, after all, the answer is simply that the bird has a prodigious sense of fun.

9

The Nightingale

The singer of such pain and bliss;
All other birds sing from their throats,
But from her heart come this bird's notes.

W. H. Davies (1871–1940)

The nightingale is a bird most people feel they know and yet surprisingly few have ever heard its song in the wild and even fewer
have managed to see one. The last part of its name comes from the
Saxon word 'galan' to sing. Not everyone realises that the bird sings
as much by day as by night. John Clare on a visit to London from
his Northamptonshire village found that the cockneys had got it all
wrong; but I doubt whether that greatly surprised him:

Your Londoners are very fond of talking about the bird and I believe
fancy every bird they hear after sunset a Nightingale. I remember while I
was there last, while walking with a friend in the fields of Shacklwell, we
saw a gentleman and lady listening very attentive by the side of a shrubbery
and when we came up we heard them lavishing praises on the beautiful
song of the nightingale which happened to be a thrush. But it did for them
and they listened and repeated their praise with heartfelt satisfaction while
the bird seemed to know the grand distinction that its song had gained for
it and strove exultingly to keep up the deception by attempting a varied
and more louder song. The dews was ready to fall, but the lady was heedless of the wet grass though the setting sun, as a traveller glad to rest, was
leaning his enlarged rim on the earth like a table of fire and lessening by
degrees out of sight leaving night and a few gilt clouds behind him. Such
is the ignorance of Nature in large Citys that are nothing less than over-
grown prisons that shut out the world and all its beautys.

John Clare (1793–1864): from 'The Prose of John Clare'

124

The Nightingale

It seems to me that part of the fascination of studying birdlife is that so many mysteries always remain unanswered and I am happy to say that no one really knows exactly why the nightingale sings at night. It is known that the males arrive from their winter quarters in tropical Africa about mid-April and that the females follow ten days later. That is when the cock birds give their virtuoso performances, vying with each other to attract a mate.

I shall always remember the sounds that filled the warm, soft night air in early May, when Nan and I used to spend holidays by the side of the broad River Rhône at Avignon. We used to stay at a small hotel 'Le Vieux Moulin' which looked straight across at the Castle of the Popes on the far bank. The wooded slopes all around were stiff with nightingales, which sang almost ceaselessly day and night. The floodlit, mediaeval building wreathed in mist looked an enchanted place and the night was full of music.

And yet even more magical can be the sound of one distant bird in the stillness of an English summer's night. Arriving at the Suffolk cottage at about three in the morning, following late news duty at the BBC's Television Centre, it was sheer poetry on getting out of the car to pause and hear those first tremulous notes, throbbing against a background murmur of the sea. In 1751, another benighted traveller penned these lines:

The Happy Nightingale

The nightingale, in dead of night,
On some green hawthorn hid from sight,
   Her wondrous art displays;
While all the feathered choir's at rest,
Nor fowler's snares her joys molest,
   She sings melodious lays.

The groves her warbling notes repeat,
The silence makes her music sweet,
   And heightens every note.
Benighted travellers admire
To hear her thus exert her fire,
   And swell her little throat.

Anon.

The anonymous poet, like so many others, overlooked the fact that it is the cock nightingale that does the singing. The favoured site near me is in thickets bordering the edge of mixed woodland, where trees give way to reed-beds which stretch away to the sea. Nothing can have changed greatly here since the days of Hereward-the-Wake. I was curious to see the nightingale, so one May morning I left my pointer Tess at home for once, and waited quietly, though uncomfortably, among brambles and blackthorn until I could trace the source of those marvellous notes. They cannot be mistaken: such perfect phrasing, such strength and purity of tone. This nightingale sang with true authority as though it knew no one could challenge it and indeed all the other birds seemed stilled in admiration.

I spent over an hour tracing that bird and endured many a scratch. When I did finally see him, it seemed hard to believe that such a flood of sound could be coming from that tiny frame. Just a small brown bird, its feathers ruffled in the wind. Its underneath was greyish-white with pale-buff colour on the breast and a russet-coloured tail, almost like a redstart. The wide open beak and swelling throat showed the fervour and intensity of his performance: the whole bird was quivering, he was singing his heart out amidst a tangle of greenery. His eye was bright and dark like a robin's. Unfortunately, he soon sensed I was there and dropped down into deep under-growth and was away.

I had taken all that time to pinpoint him because the nightingale, like the redstart and some warblers, is a bit of a ventriloquist. Perhaps this enables him to control a larger territory than he other-wise could: his voice seems to be everywhere and this also makes him difficult to find.

Professor Alfred Newton in his *Dictionary of Birds* summed up the effect of the nightingale's song as: '. . . indescribable and though several attempts from the time of Aristophanes have been made to express in syllables the sound of its many notes, its effect on those that hear it depends so much on their personal disposition as to be as varied as are its tones.'

That lovable seventeenth-century angler and philosopher Izaak Walton thought it miraculous music:

But the Nightingale (another of my Airy Creatures) breathes such sweet

loud music out of her little instrumental throat, that it might make mankind to think Miracles are not ceased. He that at midnight (when the very labourer sleeps securely) should hear (as I have very often) the clear airs, the sweet descants, the natural rising and falling, the doubling and redoubling of her voice, might well be lifted above earth, and say: 'Lord, what Musick hast thou provided for the Saints in Heaven, when thou affordest bad men such musick on Earth!'

Coleridge agreed and had no patience whatever with the idea that the nightingale is a melancholy bird. He blamed this notion on rejected lovers who mooned about thinking only of their own misery:

> A melancholy bird! Oh! idle thought!
> In Nature there is nothing melancholy.
> But some night-wandering man whose heart was pierced
> With the remembrance of a grievous wrong,
> Or slow distemper, or neglected love,
> (And so, poor wretch! filled all things with himself,
> And made all gentle sounds tell back the tale
> Of his own sorrow,) he, and such as he,
> First named those notes a melancholy strain.
> And many a poet echoes the conceit.
> *Samuel Taylor Coleridge (1772–1834): extract from 'The Nightingale'*

Certainly, no bird has been a greater source of inspiration to poets and they differ greatly about the character of the song. The ancient legend about the tragic Philomela, daughter of Pandion, the King of Athens, who was changed by the gods into a nightingale, has probably given rise to many of the melancholy interpretations – so great was her sorrow that she sang pressing her breast against a thorn. Richard Barnfield, a contemporary of Shakespeare, made use of the old superstition, although not taking it too seriously:

> As it fell upon a day
> In the merry month of May,
> Sitting in a pleasant shade
> Which a grove of myrtles made,
> Beasts did leap, and birds did sing,
> Trees did grow, and plants did spring;
> Everything did banish moan,
> Save the nightingale alone:

The Nightingale

She, poor bird, as all forlorn,
Leaned her breast up-till a thorn,
And there sung the dolefull'st ditty,
That to hear it was great pity:
'Fie, fie, fie,' now would she cry;
'Teru, teru!' by-and-bye;
That to hear her so complain,
Scarce I could from tears refrain;
For her griefs, so lively shown,
Made me think upon mine own.
Ah, thought I, thou mourn'st in vain!
None take pity on thy pain:
Senseless trees, they cannot hear thee;
Ruthless bears, they will not cheer thee.
All thy fellow-birds do sing,
Careless of thy sorrowing.
Even so, poor bird, like thee,
None alive will pity me.

Richard Barnfield (1574–1627): from 'Poems: in Divers Humours, An Ode'

Matthew Arnold was one of those who thought of the nightingale as a tragic bird and on hearing it once singing beside the Thames remembered the old Greek legend:

Hark! ah, the nightingale!
The tawny-throated!
Hark! from that moonlit cedar what a burst!
What triumph! hark – what pain!

O wanderer from a Grecian shore,
Still, after many years, in distant lands,
Still nourishing in thy bewilder'd brain
That wild, unquench'd deep-sunken, old-world pain –
Say, will it never heal?

And can this fragrant lawn
With its cool trees, and night,
And the sweet, tranquil Thames,
And moonshine, and the dew,
To thy rack'd heart and brain
Afford no balm?

Matthew Arnold (1822–1888): extract from 'Philomela'

A Celebration of Birds

Some years later Edmund Gosse also heard an errant nightingale singing in London, even though it wasn't in Berkeley Square:

Not within a granite pass,
Dim with flowers and soft with grass
Nay, but doubly, trebly sweet
In a poplared London street,
While below my windows go
Noiseless barges, to and fro,
    Through the night's calm deep,
Ah! what breaks the bonds of sleep?

No steps on the pavement fall,
Soundless swings the dark canal;
From a church-tower out of sight
Clangs the central hour of night.
Hark! the Dorian nightingale!
Pan's voice melted to a wail!
    Such another bird
Attic Tereus never heard.

Hung above the gloom and stain –
London's squalid cope of pain –
Pure as starlight, bold as love,
Honouring our scant poplar-grove,
That most heavenly voice of earth
Thrills in passion, grief or mirth,
    Laves our poison'd air
Life's best song-bath crystal-fair.

While the starry minstrel sings
Little matters what he brings,
Be it sorrow, be it pain,
Let him sing and sing again,
Till, with dawn, poor souls rejoice,
Wakening, once to hear his voice,
    Ere afar he flies,
Bound for purer woods and skies.

Edmund Gosse (1849–1928): 'Philomel in London'

The Nightingale

Christina Rossetti was one who felt the song might well be caused through joy:

> Hark! that's the nightingale,
> Telling the selfsame tale
> Her song told when this ancient earth was young:
> So echoes answered when her song was sung
> In the first wooded vale.
>
> We call it love and pain
> The passion of her strain;
> And yet we little understand or know;
> Why should it not be rather joy that so
> Throbs in each throbbing vein?
>
> *Christina Rossetti (1830–1894): 'Pain or Joy'*

Wordsworth, like his great friend Coleridge, had no doubts at all – the nightingale is a merry bird:

> O Nightingale! thou surely art
> A creature of a 'fiery heart': –
> These notes of thine – they pierce and pierce;
> Tumultuous harmony and fierce!
> Thou sing'st as if the God of wine
> Had helped thee to a Valentine;
> A song in mockery and despite
> Of shades, and dews, and silent night;
> And steady bliss, and all the loves
> Now sleeping in these peaceful groves.
>
> *William Wordsworth (1770–1850): 'Poems of Imagination'*

The song is heard only until mid-June, that is until the young are hatched. It is certain that wherever the nightingale chooses to breed there will always be thick undergrowth. The nest is usually just a few inches above the ground and often placed among dead leaves of oak or Spanish chestnut. As dead oak leaves are also the main building material, the nest blends perfectly with its surroundings. The usual number of eggs is five. They are olive-brown in colour. There is only one brood. The eggs merge into their background; yet Tennyson found perfect words for them when he wrote:

The music of the moon
Sleeps in the plain eggs of the nightingale.

Once the young are hatched, the parent birds lose all their shyness as they set determinedly about the all-important job of feeding their nestlings. It is then, in their frantic dashes to and from the nest, beaks crammed with insect food, that a totally different sound is heard; no melodious song but a harsh, peevish, croak of alarm may greet you should you stray anywhere near the nest.

Apart from the marvel of its song, there is the mystery of the bird's distribution. For some reason, it seldom ventures north or west of a line drawn between the Humber and the Severn and scarcely ever visits Wales. In the last century, Richard Jefferies, like many nature writers before and since, found this most puzzling. And as for Scotland:

It seems, for instance, to have as great a dislike to Scotland as Dr. Johnson himself. This is not on account of the cold; for it visits much colder countries. Indeed, climate has much less influence with it than one might expect in the case of the summer immigrant. It chooses rather to ignore Devonshire and Cornwall, and seems to hold, with the great lexicographer, that Ireland is worth seeing but not worth going to see. It rarely goes there, though it is not correct to say that it is never to be met with. Its appreciation of Yorkshire is extremely arbitrary. In some parts it is often to be met with; in others its occurrence is very rare. A few years ago a nightingale came to a wood in the neighbourhood of one of the large manufacturing towns. The intelligence was soon noised about, and the wood got to be so popular that an enterprising omnibus proprietor started a vehicle that took passengers 'to the Nightingale', at sixpence a head. The bird soon left that wood, and a little boy who got up into a tree and imitated it, was very near being stoned in the moonlight by some angry passengers who were disappointed at the failure of their excursion.

Richard Jefferies (1848–1887): 'Chronicles of the Hedges'

In fact nightingales do in some years venture to Scotland. Such a year was 1826. It was apparently a hot, dry summer and Robert Dick Duncan remembered hearing the unmistakable song in Calder Wood, Midlothian:

Before about midnight, while the full moon shone bright and clear, the superior warble of the male was first heard, which soon attracted a number of admiring individuals, who hastened to the spot, supposing it at first to be an escaped canary. The owner of the wood was extremely anxious to preserve them, thinking that they might perhaps propagate; but with all his care and attention, some malicious and selfish individuals attempted to take them with bird lime, but failing in their efforts, they afterwards shot the male, upon which the female left the wood.

But there is proof in the BBC Archives that at least one nightingale took a more favourable view of Scotland than did Dr Johnson. Its song was recorded at Stirling Castle, of all places, in 1952. I know this is so because I have had the pleasure of playing it over the air in a BBC programme. It is true the bird did sound somewhat hesitant north of the border; perhaps it had heard of the fate of some of its predecessors.

But why I wonder should the nightingale be so wedded to the south-eastern counties of England? Again, nobody really knows. It may be something to do with rainfall, as the nightingale is not over fond of damp places, although its favourite haunts may often be close by a stream or river.

Sadly, there has been a marked reduction in their numbers especially over the past thirty years or so. On the famous Minsmere Reserve of the RSPB, a few miles down the coast from my cottage, whereas in 1959 there were at least fifty pairs, today there are less than half that number. None of these nests is within a mile of the coast. My old friend Herbert Axell, who was in charge of the Reserve for sixteen years, is convinced that this is due to the succession of cold springs we have had in recent years. Temperature must certainly be an important factor, as it affects the availability of insects on which the nightingales depend for food. What a tragic loss it will be if the nightingales' numbers continue to decline.

At least today there are Wild Bird Protection Acts and nightingales no longer end up in cages. Richard Jefferies remembered the bad old days before 1880 when the first Act was passed:

A couple of roughs would come down from town and silence a whole grove. The nightingale would watch the trap being laid, and pounce on the alluring mealworm as soon as the trapper was out of sight. It would be quite as much curiosity as gluttony that led to its fate; and the fate was a sad one. These birds are so shy that it is nearly impossible to keep them alive. They literally beat themselves to death against their prison wires. So for the first fortnight of captivity the wings were tied, and the bird was kept caged in the dark. Light was gradually let in – at first by a few pin-holes in the paper that covered the cage. The captive would peck and peck at these till a rent was made and in time the paper could come away. The mortality was pitiable. Seventy per cent of these little creatures that were singing a week before in full-throated ease in the Surrey lanes would be flung out into the gutters of Seven Dials or Whitechapel.

Richard Jefferies (1848–1887): 'Chronicles of the Hedges'

Some of those very same birds may well have been trapped in that part of the county as described in 1900:

In a side-glen of the Surrey Hills, running down to the deep stream of the River Wey, lies the Nightingale Valley. Two tiny streams cut their way down the steep and sandy hills, and unite in a pool which almost fills the bottom of the hollow. The cock-birds usually arrive in the valley at the end of the second week in April, and spend at least a week in practising and recalling their song. At such times they are extremely tame, and the writer has often watched from a few yards' distance the singer, who shows far less nervousness in practising before a stranger than is often observed in human vocalists. The first long-drawn notes are commonly run through without difficulty, but the subsequent trills and changes can no more be acquired without practice and training by the nightingale than by a human singer.

C. J. Cornish: 'Wild England of Today'

Reading a passage like this is to realise how steeply their numbers have declined since the turn of the century. What a price to pay for progress. Each year about 70,000 acres of our countryside disappear under concrete, much of it for motorways. On that basis, a county the size of Bedfordshire vanishes every four years. How many more wild groves beloved of nightingales must be flattened by the bull-dozers?

> And I know a grove
> Of large extent, hard by a castle huge,
> Which the great lord inhabits not; and so
> This grove is wild with tangling underwood,
> And the trim walks are broken up, and grass,
> Thin grass and king-cups, grow within the paths,

But never elsewhere in one place I knew
So many nightingales; and far and near,
In wood and thicket, over the wide grove,
They answer and provoke each other's songs,
With skirmish and capricious passagings,
And murmurs musical and swift jug-jug;
And one, low piping, sounds more sweet than all,
Stirring the air with such an harmony,
That should you close your eyes, you might almost
Forget it was not day. On moonlight bushes,
Whose dewy leaflets are but half disclosed,
You may perchance behold them on the twigs,
Their bright, bright eyes, their eyes both bright and full,
Glistening, while many a glow-worm in the shade
Lights up her love-torch.
Samuel Taylor Coleridge (1772–1834): extract from 'The Nightingale'

William Cowper's 'Glow-worm' very nearly ended up as a nightingale's supper:

A Nightingale that all day long
Had cheered the village with his song,
Nor yet at eve his note suspended,
Nor yet when eventide was ended,
Began to feel, as well he might,
The keen demands of appetite;
When looking eagerly around,
He spied far off, upon the ground,
A something shining in the dark,
And knew the Glow-worm by his spark;
So, stooping down from hawthorn top,
He thought to put him in his crop.
The worm, aware of his intent,
Harangued him thus, right eloquent:
'Did you admire my lamp,' quoth he,
'As much as I your minstrelsy,
You would abhor to do me wrong,
As much as I to spoil your song:
For 'twas the self-same Power Divine
Taught you to sing, and me to shine:

> That you with music, I with light,
> Might beautify and cheer the night.'
> The songster heard this short oration,
> And warbling out his approbation,
> Released him, as my story tells,
> And found a supper somewhere else.
> *William Cowper (1731–1800): 'The Nightingale and the Glow-worm'*

Of course there will always be some to whom the sound of the nightingale is not entirely welcome. This unsigned letter from the Home Counties appeared in *Wild Country Life* for 20 April 1901:

More than one of the sheltered gardens in this neighbourhood might have been the scene of the story in which the visitor from London littered the lawn with missiles from his bedroom during the night, and came down to breakfast complaining of the 'beastly birds that would not let him get a wink of sleep'.

What torment to suffer a surfeit of nightingales.

F. O. Morris in his *A History of British Birds* after eulogising about the nightingale's vocal accomplishments – adds cryptically: 'It has been known to imitate the human voice.'

Certainly, that eminent sixteenth-century ornithologist Willoughby recounted in his Book II a very strange happening indeed. It came to him in the form of a despatch from a 'very learned and credible person' who had apparently been staying at a small inn in Germany:

Because you are writing of Birds, I will tell you something concerning Nightingales . . . wonderful and almost incredible, but yet most true, and which I myself heard with these ears, and had experience of, this last Diet of Ratisbone in the year 1546 whilst I lodged there in a common Inn at the sign of the Golden Crown. Our Host had three Nightingales, placed separately, so that each was shut up singly by itself in a dark Cage. It happened that at that time, being the Spring of the year, when those birds are wont to sing indefatigably, and almost incessantly: I was so afflicted with the Stone, that I could sleep very little all night. Then about and after Midnight, when there was no noise in the house, but all was still, you might have heard strange janglings, and emulations of two Nightingales, talking one with another, and plainly imitating men's discourses. For my part I was almost astonished with wonder. For they in the night-season, when all was whist and quiet, in conference together produced and repeated whatever they had heard in the day time from the Guests talking together, and had thought upon. Those two of them which were most notable, and masters of this Art, were scarce ten foot distant one from the other: the third hung more remote, so that I could not so well hear it as I lay in bed. But those two, it is wonderful to tell, how they provoked one another and by answering invited and drew one another to speak. Yet did they not confound their words, talking both together, but rather utter them alternately, or by course. But besides the daily discourse, which they had lately heard of the Guests, they did chant out especially two stories one to another, for a long time, even from Midnight till Morning, so long as there was no noise of men stirring, and that with that native modulation and inflection of their notes, that no man, unless he were very attentive and headful, would either have expected from those little Creatures, or easily observed. When I asked the Host, whether their Tongues had been slit, or they taught to speak anything? He answered no; whether he had observed or did understand what they sung in the night? He likewise denied that. The same said the whole Family. But I who could not sleep whole nights together did greedily and attentively hearken to the birds, greatly indeed admiring their industry and contention. One of their stories was concerning the Tapster, or House-knight (as they call them) and his Wife, who refused to follow him going into the Wars, as he desired her. For the Husband, endeavoured to persuade his wife, as far as I understand by those birds, in hope of prey, that she would leave her service in that Inn, and go along with him into the Wars. But she, refusing to follow him, did resolve either to stay at Ratisbone, or go away to Nurenberg. For there had been an earnest and long contention between them about this matter, but (as far as I understand) no body being present besides, and without the privity of the Master of the House, and all this Dialogue the birds repeated. And if by chance in their wrangling they cast forth any unseemly words, and that ought rather to have been suppressed and kept secret, the Birds, as not knowing the difference between modest and immodest, honest and filthy words, did out with them . . .

Gossiping nightingales swearing in German. The mind boggles. What can the poor chap have had as a nightcap!

And then how strange and incongruous it must have seemed to hear the immortal bird singing amid the death and destruction of the Great War. A Mr M. V. B. Hill wrote to *The Times*, on 4 June 1977, still remembering the nightingales singing sixty years before while he waited for the attack on the Messines Ridge: 'This was on

June 7th. They were about one mile behind the front line and there seemed to be a nightingale in every bush singing at the top of his lungs, until the largest mine of the war went off and the battle began at 3.10 a.m.'

Last year in early summer Nan and I made our first visit to Rome. It was stuffy and humid. For some days the sirocco had been bringing to the eternal city the hot breath of Africa, even depositing some of the sand from the desert on once shining limousines. We trudged round the Pantheon, St Peter's, the Sistine Chapel and the Vatican Museum. We gazed at the Trevi Fountain and the Spanish Steps and a thousand things besides. Then we came upon an oasis of coolness and calm. The English cemetery nestles close by the ancient city wall in the shadow of a great, white pyramid brought from Egypt to commemorate some Roman triumph. Great cypresses lend their shade and many other trees and flowers make it a place of quiet enchantment. Here lies all that was mortal of John Keats. There have been countless tributes to the nightingale but none for me has more magic or potency than his:

> My heart aches, and a drowsy numbness pains
>   My sense, as though of hemlock I had drunk,
> Or emptied some dull opiate to the drains
>   One minute past, and Lethe-wards had sunk:
> 'Tis not through envy of thy happy lot,
>   But being too happy in thy happiness, –
>   That thou, light-winged Dryad of the trees,
>   In some melodious plot
>   Of beechen green, and shadows numberless,
>   Singest of summer in full-throated ease.
>
> O, for a draught of vintage! that hath been
>   Cool'd a long age in the deep-delved earth,
> Tasting of Flora and the country green,
>   Dance, and Provençal song, and sunburnt mirth!
> O for a beaker full of the warm South,
>   Full of the true, the blushful Hippocrene,
>   With beaded bubbles winking at the brim,
>   And purple-stained mouth;
>   That I might drink, and leave the world unseen,
>   And with thee fade away into the forest dim:

The Nightingale

Fade far away, dissolve, and quite forget
    What thou among the leaves hast never known,
The weariness, the fever, and the fret
    Here, where men sit and hear each other groan;
Where palsy shakes a few, sad, last gray hairs,
      Where youth grows pale, and spectre-thin, and dies;
        Where but to think is to be full of sorrow
          And leaden-eyed despairs;
      Where Beauty cannot keep her lustrous eyes,
      Or new Love pine at them beyond to-morrow.

Away! away! for I will fly to thee,
    Not charioted by Bacchus and his pards,
But on the viewless wings of Poesy,
    Though the dull brain perplexes and retards:
Already with thee! tender is the night,
      And haply the Queen-Moon is on her throne,
        Cluster'd around by all her starry Fays;
          But here there is no light,
Save what from heaven is with the breezes blown
    Through verdurous glooms and winding mossy ways.

I cannot see what flowers are at my feet,
    Nor what soft incense hangs upon the boughs,
But, in embalmed darkness, guess each sweet
    Wherewith the seasonable month endows
The grass, the thicket, and the fruit-tree wild;
      White hawthorn, and the pastoral eglantine;
        Fast fading violets cover'd up in leaves;
          And mid-May's eldest child,
The coming musk-rose, full of dewy wine,
    The murmurous haunt of flies on summer eves.

Darkling I listen; and for many a time
    I have been half in love with easeful Death,
Call'd him soft names in many a mused rhyme,
    To take into the air my quiet breath;
Now more than ever seems it rich to die,
    To cease upon the midnight with no pain,
      While thou art pouring forth thy soul abroad
        In such an ecstasy!
Still wouldst thou sing, and I have ears in vain –
    To thy high requiem become a sod.

Thou wast not born for death, immortal Bird!
   No hungry generations tread thee down;
The voice I hear this passing night was heard
   In ancient days by emperor and clown:
Perhaps the self-same song that found a path
     Through the sad heart of Ruth, when, sick for home,
       She stood in tears amid the alien corn;
        The same that oft-times hath
Charm'd magic casements, opening on the foam
   Of perilous seas, in faery lands forlorn.

   Forlorn! the very word is like a bell
     To toll me back from thee to my sole self!
   Adieu! the fancy cannot cheat so well
     As she is fam'd to do, deceiving elf.
   Adieu! adieu! thy plaintive anthem fades
     Past the near meadows, over the still stream,
       Up the hill-side; and now 'tis buried deep
        In the next valley-glades:
   Was it a vision, or a waking dream?
   Fled is that music: – Do I wake or sleep?

John Keats (1795–1821)

10

The Swan

The stately-sailing swan
Gives out his snowy plumage to the gale,
And, arching proud his neck, with oary feet
Bears forward fierce, and guards his osier-isle,
Protective of his young.
James Thomson (1700–1748): 'The Seasons'

Stop someone at random in a city street, ask him or her to name a dozen British birds, and the chances are that the swan would be among them. This is hardly surprising, it's an adornment to be seen throughout the year in all parts of the country – on lakes and estuaries, rivers and reservoirs or on ponds in the parks:

She is pleasing to all eyes, and is decorative, embellishing all places she frequents; she is liked, praised and admired: no species merits this more. Nature has not in fact endowed any others with as many noble and gentle graces, which remind us of its most charming works: an elegant figure, rounded forms, graceful contours, a dazzling and pure white, easy and expressive movements with attitudes that are now animated and then left in quiet abandon.
Comte de Buffon (1707–1788): 'Le Cygne' from 'Oeuvres'

My own attachment to swans began early on – when I was about four. The occasion was a family picnic party at a Surrey beauty spot, Keston Ponds. It was in the days when a drive in a motor car was not only a pleasure but an event. An indulgent uncle had become the proud possessor of a new green Wolseley tourer with gleaming brass headlamps and a delicious smell of leather inside.

We set out that morning from Croydon, I hoping fervently that some of my little friends in the neighbourhood might witness me riding ensconced in such splendour. There was only one gratifying moment and I waved like mad, but for the most part my acquaintances were maddeningly absent.

Apart from torment by wasps, lunch, spread on rugs among the heather and gorse, was a huge delight. There was almost half a cottage loaf left over and about a hundred yards away I espied some swans sailing regally on a tussocky mere. In no time, I was heading in their direction, clutching my offering of bread. For some reason, I was wearing new black lace-up boots which squeaked horribly. Never had I seen such green, luscious grass. The next moment it was swallowing me up. Black mud sucking and squelching all round. Soon it was over my knees and I was still going down. Fortunately, I must have yelled to good effect because rescue was at hand. Then, an undignified return home with my lower half swathed in newspapers to keep the mud off the Wolseley.

Fifty-six years later, when I retired from the News desk, and BBC TV's 'Nationwide' invited me to become their wildlife reporter, the first feature I did for them was, as it happened, on the subject of swans. It was mid-winter and from London with the camera crew I headed for the Fens. This was the place where I knew we were certain to see the three species of European swan: the familiar resident mute swan and the two winter visitors – the Bewick's and the whooper.

Rain was unrelenting as we drove through Ely, where Hereward-the-Wake once held out against the Normans, until they managed to build a road to it across the marshes. Here too centuries later Oliver Cromwell lived with his family. The superb cathedral with its octagonal lantern tower has gazed over the flat land around it since 1083. At Littleport, where the River Ouse runs through the town, there had been rioting when attempts were made to drain the Fens over three hundred years ago. Five men were hanged and many more transported to the colonies. Fenmen were not called 'fen-tigers' for nothing: like the high water, their tempers were hard to keep in check.

The only corpses we saw that day were those of moles impaled on a strand of barbed wire bordering a field. There were eight of them with pinkish-white paws raised in supplication. At Wisbech the narrow road suddenly becomes dead straight, pulled taut, as it runs well above the level of the fields of black earth all around.

This is some of Britain's richest agricultural land but it is being eroded fast. As an indicator, a long post was banged into a field at Holme Fen in 1851, until only the tip of it showed above ground. Since then, fourteen-and-a-half feet of topsoil has gone and the post points today like a warning finger. Only a few feet of rich black earth now remain. Many inches of it seemed to have spread over onto the road as our car churned through a morass of mud. All around were the Ouse Washes, the greatest stretch of regularly flooded marshland left in Britain.

The Romans were the first to attempt drainage here and the Normans after them. The Vikings came to harry and raid, but this great swamp remained largely isolated until the seventeenth century when Francis, the fourth Earl of Bedford, invited the Dutchman Cornelius Vermuyden to undertake the work of drainage in a big way.

First he cut a dyke running straight for over twenty miles which was called the Old Bedford River. This failed to hold the floodwaters so a second cut, the New Bedford, was made half a mile away and parallel to it. The area in between is grazed in summer and floods in winter, forming one of the most important refuges for wildfowl in the whole of Europe.

Not surprisingly, three important conservation bodies have acquired holdings here: the RSPB, the Cambridgeshire and Isle of Ely Naturalists' Trust, and the Wildfowl Trust at Welney. This was ideal for our purposes as the Trust has a splendid hide with great windows looking out on to a wide lagoon. While the cameras were being set up, I talked to the warden, a fen-tiger himself, Josh Scott. He is the perfect example of a hunter turned conservationist. As a youngster, he became one of the 'wash shepherds' looking after the cattle grazed there from May to September. In winter to retain their services the local farmers gave the shepherds shooting rights.

At one time, with huge punt-guns thousands of duck and plovers were shot and sent to London for sale. After war service, Josh found it difficult to make a living in the Washes and was on the point of leaving when he happily met Sir Peter Scott, who was trying to set up a wildfowl refuge there. Josh soon sold his gun, bought binoculars and settled in happily as warden. He says that taking the job was the best thing he ever did.

Nearest to our cameras were several family parties of smallish swans with black and yellow bills. These were Bewick's, named after the famous eighteenth-century engraver Thomas Bewick. Their breeding grounds are in the uninhabited tundra regions of Arctic Russia stretching from the Kola Peninsula to Eastern Siberia. The small grey cygnets had somehow managed to make the two-thousand-mile flight with their parents, even though they can only have been four or five months old when they started. A flight of deadly danger from the weather, to say nothing of the barrage of lead shot from wildfowlers; quite an achievement.

Many of the same individuals return here each year and they can be recognised from the yellow and black markings on their bills. By the time they are eighteen months old, the pattern is formed and remains for life. So experts can readily identify each swan, as no two have the same pattern.

On another part of the lagoon were some larger swans with necks as straight as walking sticks. Their bills were longer than the Bewick's and the yellow markings extended further down the bill ending in a point. These were whooper swans which had flown in recently from Iceland where they breed in the pine forests and shallow lakes. Many of them I noticed had a rust-coloured stain on heads and necks and Josh explained that this was due to the iron compounds present in Icelandic lakes and streams. In a month or two they would lose the stain after feeding in our waters which are free of them.

Nearby were groups of familiar British mute swans among their wilder cousins. With graceful, arched necks and bright orange bills they looked quite homely. The males or cobs are easily distinguished from the pens by the pronounced black nobs just below the forehead.

In this concourse of hundreds of swans, the small Bewick's were in the majority. There must have been some anxiety among them about keeping their family parties together, as I noticed continual neck-bobbing going on, which is one way they communicate. Towards late afternoon more swans flew in and, as soon as they had

landed on the water with exquisite grace, the first thing they did was to drink. These were birds which had been feeding during the day on the black fenlands around and their beaks, and throats, were dirty and no doubt very dry.

The light was fading fast and soon came the magical moment when the carefully concealed floodlighting was switched on. Suddenly it was a scene of luminous beauty, as we gazed in silent admiration at this true swan lake. Above, in the night sky, we heard the wild chorus of swans calling, their voices sharp and clear on the frosty air. Welney in mid-winter affords some of the most memorable wildlife sights and sounds to be experienced anywhere in the world.

We have looked briefly at the three European swans but for most of us in Britain and throughout our history and literature, it is the resident mute swan that we chiefly celebrate.

On the dykes between my Suffolk cottage and the sea, each year, there is a family of swans. Often I come upon them suddenly on rounding a bend in the stream, or glimpse them unexpectedly through a gap in the reeds. Always, I feel an immense sense of privilege at seeing their stately procession. Tess, my pointer, comes close to heel so as not to disturb them.

Wordsworth painted the perfect portrait and noted how the female often carries the tiny cygnets, allowing them to snuggle under her wings or sit on her back:

> He swells his lifted chest, and backward flings
> His bridling neck between his tow'ring wings;
> Stately, and burning in his pride, divides,
> And glorying looks around, the silent tides:
> On as he floats, the silver'd waters glow,
> Proud of the varying arch and moveless form of snow.
> While tender Cares and mild domestic Loves
> With furtive watch pursue her as she moves,
> The female with a meeker charm succeeds,
> And her brown little ones around her leads,
> Nibbling the water lilies as they pass,
> Or playing wanton with the floating grass:
> She in a mother's care, her beauty's pride
> Forgets, unweary'd watching every side,

The Swan

She calls them near, and with affection sweet
Alternately relieves their weary feet;
Alternately they mount her back, and rest,
Close by her mantling wings' embraces prest.
William Wordsworth (1770–1850): 'From an Evening Walk'

Nearer our own time, Edmund Blunden also catches marvellously the sense of wonder at suddenly coming upon a company of swans. He contrasts their age-old serenity with man's fever and fret. He wrote these lines during the war:

Walking the river way to change our note
From the hard season and from harder care,
    Marvelling we found the swans,
The swans on sullen swollen dykes afloat
Or moored on tussocks, a full company there,
White breasts and necks, advance and poise and stir
Filling the scene, while rays of steel and bronze
From the far dying sun touched the dead reeds.

So easy was the manner of each one,
So sure and wise the course of all their needs,
So free their unity, in that level sun
And floodland tipped with sedge and osiery,
It might have been where man was yet to be,
Some mere where none but swans were ever kings,
Where gulls might hunt, a wide flight in from sea,
And page-like small birds come: all innocent wings.

O picture of some first divine intent,
O young world which perhaps was modelled thus,
    Where even hard winter meant
No disproportion, hopeless hungers none,
And set no task which could not well be done.
Now this primeval pattern gleamed at us
Right near the town's black smoke-towers and the roar
Of trains bearing the sons of man to war.
Edmund Blunden (1896–): 'A Prospect of Swans' from 'Poems of Many Years'

How lovely it must be to have one's own swans. Derek Neville, a Norfolk writer and philosopher who died recently, lived at

Itteringham Mill, which stands astride the river between Norwich and the sea. His favourite view was down-stream, where the river curves and reedy water-meadows stretch away to the sea. There the birds reigned supreme, especially the swans. He describes how he and his wife used to feel as they saw the swans suddenly rounding the bend:

Serene, poised, royal in their very natures – they come sailing into sight, knowing that the river is their kingdom, their heaven, their true environment. And the sight of them kindles something in one, for it is as though they choose to cross the boundary between their world and ours. True, we feed them, but they lose no dignity in the process. They bestow their presence upon us – while we can only give them bits of bread. They glide without apparent effort up to the mill-pond and there they will spend an hour or two – sometimes a whole day, quietly feeding, smoothing their feathers, keeping an eye open for food or resting upon the surface of the water, often with one leg tucked up against a wing – like a spare oar. Sometimes they are still there long after dark, like dear ghostly shapes, silent and friendly; or sometimes the moonlight spills over them, or the mist rises from the river about them, as though the very elements strive to provide a fitting background to the magic of their presence.

Derek Neville and especially his wife came to love the swans.

One autumn the swans deserted them and were greatly missed, so as Christmas drew near, the presents he and the children bought for his wife tended to be on the theme of swans. When the great morning came, gifts were happily exchanged and the family duly came downstairs to breakfast:

And there, with all of us present, it happened! From the kitchen window which looks out upon the river, one of us pointed to the distant bend. And before our astonished eyes, sailing in majestic convoy, one after another, came no less than nine swans, gleaming with purity, proud and purposeful. Right up to our pool they came – as though they'd had a message asking them to present themselves at that precise moment. They perfected our tiny gifts. They filled our morning with wondrous joy. And we shall always look back upon that experience with the knowledge that there are indeed more things in heaven and on earth than are dreamed of in most philosophies.

Extract from 'The Swans', written and published by Derek Neville

But life is not always idyllic even for swans. They have occasional territorial battles and a formidable sight it must be to see two cobs joined in mortal combat. There are few sadder sights than a dead swan:

> Midstream they met. Challenger and champion,
> They fought a war for honour
> Fierce, sharp, but with no honour:
> Each had a simple aim and sought it quickly.
> The combat over the victor sailed away
> Broken, but placid as is the gift of swans,
> Leaving his rival to his shame alone.
> I listened for a song, according to story,
> But this swan's death was out of character –
> No giving up of the grace of life
> In a sad lingering music.
> I saw the beaten swan rise on the water
> As though to outreach pain, its webbed feet
> Banging the river helplessly, its wings
> Loose in a last hysteria. Then the neck
> Was floating like a rope and the swan was dead.
> It drifted away and all around it swan's-down
> Bobbed on the river like children's little boats.
> *Clifford Dyment (1914–): 'The Swans' from 'Collected Poems'*

A most remarkable battle was recorded in the editorial column of *Country Life* for 29 April 1899:

The ornamental water at Syon House, which was illustrated recently in the pages of Country Life, has been the scene of a curious encounter between a voracious fish and a mute swan, which had an unfortunate and fatal ending for the latter. A correspondent, in sending the details of the battle royal which raged between the two, remarks that he thinks a record of the occurrence will be interesting to our readers, and we quite agree. It seems that the bird, a fine male specimen, was quietly dipping his head beneath the water, when it was seized by an enormous fish who, notwithstanding the struggles of the swan, succeeded in keeping the head below the surface until the bird was drowned. Thereupon the fish endeavoured to swallow the bird's head, and was so engaged when the fate of the unlucky creature was thus discovered. Upon the removal of the carcase it was seen that the head of the swan was severely bitten, and it is surmised that a pike is responsible for the unusual occurrence, and that hunger provoked the attack. It is known that an enormous jack has existed in the lake for many years, and when last seen, some time ago, it was locally estimated to weigh between 40 and 50 lbs. To our knowledge the strength of the swan and the power of the pike have never before been contrasted in so singular a fashion, and the occurrence is likely to lend colour to some of the tales told by our ardent – and truthful – fishermen.

Swans have immensely powerful wings and it is often said that a swan can break a man's leg with one blow. This could be a slight exaggeration but it is certainly unwise to allow children or dogs anywhere near a nest containing eggs or cygnets.

E. L. Roberts once put it to the test himself and discovered what a terrible adversary the cob swan can be:

Years ago I thought to call the bluff of a particularly pugnacious cob, and received more than I bargained for. The pen, a billowing mass of snowy plumage, sedately brooded her six big greenish eggs in the great nest with the cob cruising nearby. As I advanced, up went his hackles in anger. His great wings were arched like sails over his back. With neck swelling to twice its normal thickness he hissed menacingly. I continued to advance steadily. The cob lowered his head and swam to meet me; he looked to be in deadly earnest. Still I advanced. He climbed stiffly from the water and stood on the bank six feet in front of me, fury trembling in every feather.

Now I would test him! I stretched out my leg and planted my foot on the side of the massive nest. The sitting pen hissed and fidgeted. Then the cob went into action. Rearing up and lashing the air with mighty wings, he rushed at me. I tried to parry him with my stick but it was swept aside like a straw as paralysing blows rained upon my legs and arms. There was absolutely no defence against the swan's attack. I was overwhelmed, engulfed by the flailing wings and driven to ignominious flight in a matter of seconds.

E. L. Roberts: extract from 'The Happy Countryman'

The mating of the noble birds is a moment of beauty and awe. It takes place when they are three or four years old and the pairs are usually faithful for life:

> Even now I wish that you had been there
> Sitting beside me on the riverbank:

The Swan

The cob and his pen sailing in rhythm
Until their small heads met and the final
Heraldic moment dissolved in ripples.

This was a marriage and a baptism,
A holding of breath, nearly a drowning,
Wings spread wide for balance where he trod,
Her feathers full of water and her neck
Under the water like a bar of light.

Michael Longley: 'Swans Mating'

It is sobering to think that mute swans were once highly prized as luxury food and were introduced and bred in England for that purpose. Some say that Richard the Lionheart brought the first swans home from Cyprus after the third crusade, but it seems likely that they were here long before that.

For centuries the Crown controlled the ownership of swans through royal swanherds and courts known as 'swanmotes'. These privately owned birds were pinioned to prevent their flying away and then nicked in the skin of the upper bill, or sometimes marked on the foot as a sign of ownership. In Queen Elizabeth I's day there were nine hundred distinctive marks recognised.

The swan-upping pageantry on the Thames in the third week of July dates back to the fifteenth century. Two City Guilds own one third of the Thames' swans. The cygnets are caught and have their bills nicked, one mark for the Dyers and two for the Vintners. All unmarked swans on the river belong to the Queen who still bears the ancient title of 'Seigneur of Swans'.

At one time there was an ingenious penalty exacted from anyone caught stealing a swan. It was a fine which had to be paid in wheat. The bird was hung in a room by the beak so that its tail feathers just touched the ground. The culprit then had to reimburse the owner by pouring wheat over the swan until it covered the bird up to the tip of its beak.

It is only over the past one hundred years or so that mute swans have been freed to become common birds breeding in the wild. No one knows why they are called mute. I recently called at the ancient swannery at Abbotsbury in Dorset which was set up by the Benedictine monks about a thousand years ago. It consists of an eight-mile-long tidal lagoon sheltered by the great shingle bank known as Chesil Beach.

Records show that in 1591 during the reign of Queen Elizabeth there were 410 swans and 90 cygnets and the average numbers are much the same today. Fred Lexter who is Keeper of the Swans there says they are not silent, as their name implies; but do utter occasional plaintive calls in spring and when swimming with their young. The great mystery is what gave rise to the legend of the death-song of the dying swan. This goes back to Greek and Roman mythology and poets have maintained the charming fiction through the ages but evidence is there none. The confusion is total as Charles Dickens observed in *Martin Chuzzlewit*:

> 'The name of those fabulous animals (pagan I regret to say) who used to sing in the water, has quite escaped me.'
> 'No,' said Mr. Pecksniff.
> 'Not swans. Very like swans, too. Thank you.'
> The nephew propounded 'Oysters.'
> 'No,' said Mr. Pecksniff, – nor oysters. But by no means unlike oysters; a very excellent idea; thank you, my dear sir, very much. Wait Sirens! Dear me! Sirens, of course.'

Sometimes though it is tempting to agree with the anonymous poet who penned these immortal lines:

> The silver swan, who living had no note,
> When death approached, unlocked her silent throat,
> Leaning her breast against the reedy shore,
> Thus sang her first and last, and sung no more:
> Farewell, all joys! O death, come close mine eyes;
> More geese than swans now live, more fools than wise.

Then of course, there is Coleridge's epigram:

> Swans sing before they die – 'twere no bad thing
> Did certain persons die before they sing.

The most thrilling sound made by the mute swan is the rhythmical music produced by its wing-beats. Many a time have I stood transfixed on a lonely shore as a flight of swans passed overhead. This marvellous, wild sound probably helps keep the flock together, much as does the constant vocal singing of the whoopers and Bewick's.

The mute swan's powerful wings can match the cruising speed of a car. A flight of them once flew level with Colin Stephens as he headed for London on the motorway. He wrote to *The Countryman* magazine: 'A flight of five mute swans appeared from the south as we were driving towards London along the M4. They crossed the motorway about 40 feet up just ahead of our car, then turned and flew level with us for nearly half a mile at a steady 58 m.p.h. before they veered north again. Their wings beat approximately twice per second.'

Only a few whoopers nest in Scotland, but when the wintering flocks fly in from Iceland the air is full of their bell-like cries. E. A. Armstrong writes of seeing some of these swans at their breeding place on one of the great lakes in Iceland set among mauve-coloured mountains:

One bird was sitting quietly on the water near the nest. In the distance I saw a white speck approaching. Flap, flap, flap, he came speeding up to his mate and alighted with a great splashing on the water. Then, facing each other, they performed a ceremony of greeting, raising their heads high, arching their wings, and uttering together a series of loud, trumpet-like calls. Gradually the excitement died down, but they went on calling, replying to one another. Swimming side by side, they bent their necks and dipped their heads together several times in succession, so that they appeared to be, not two separate birds, but a single swan reflected in a mirror.

E. A. Armstrong (1900–   ): 'The Way Birds Live'

Unlike the mute swans, whoopers seldom show any affection for man. An exception occurred in 1186 in the reign of King John when Hugh, Bishop of Witham was summoned to fill the episcopal chair at Lincoln:

Burgundian-born, Carthusian-trained, the future Saint was a very human person in whom were combined a peppery temper, a dauntless spirit, and a compassionate heart. He won the grudging respect of King John; he won the ungrudging affection of the Jews of Lincoln, a numerous community; and immediately upon his first coming to the episcopal manor at Stowe he won the devotion of a whooper swan.

It was a magnificent specimen, plumed with gold about the neck and head, and its arrival coincided with that of the Bishop himself. As he was known to be a lover of wild birds, it was brought, strangely acquiescent, into his presence. Without demur it accepted a piece of bread from his hand; and thereafter it installed itself as his friend, protector and companion. Sometimes it would thrust its head right up his long sleeve, 'as if wishing to whisper in his ear'; often it would try, with wings and beak and great clamour, to prevent anyone drawing near: nor would it suffer other swans (with one exception) to nest upon the Bishop's wide manorial waters. This exception was a pen, but she, says the old chronicle, was spared for companionship and not, it would seem, 'for the sake of progeny'.

If it perceived that the servants were making preparations for the return of the Bishop after one of his periodical absences, the swan would not only 'fly along the surface of the stream, making a great noise', but would even 'leave the water and walk with long strides either to the hall or the outer gate', as if going to welcome its master.

D. M. Stuart: from 'A Book of Birds and Beasts'

Another legend still lingers on, especially in some parts of Ireland, that souls of the departed may take possession of the body of a swan. For this reason there is a strong feeling against killing them. John Cordeaux in *British Birds with their Nests and Eggs* told this tale:

A few years ago, a wounded swan remained throughout the summer on Loch Bee, and attracted much attention by the loud and melancholy cries to which it gave utterance. An old crone, in telling me about this bird, reiterated her conviction that it was the ghost of her grandmother, who had met with a violent death about sixty years previously. It was a bold image, though I cannot but think that a Black Swan would have been more appropriate.

Perhaps it is right that a final tribute should come from 'the land of faery' – from Ireland's great mystic poet William Butler Yeats:

The Swan

The Wild Swans at Coole

The trees are in their autumn beauty,
The woodland paths are dry,
Under the October twilight the water
Mirrors a still sky;
Upon the brimming water among the stones
Are nine-and-fifty swans.

The nineteenth autumn has come upon me
Since I first made my count;
I saw, before I had well finished,
All suddenly mount
And scatter wheeling in great broken rings
Upon their clamorous wings.

I have looked upon those brilliant creatures,
And now my heart is sore.
All's changed since I, hearing at twilight,
The first time on this shore,
The bell-beat of their wings above my head,
Trod with a lighter tread.

Unwearied still, lover by lover,
They paddle in the cold,
Companionable streams or climb the air;
Their hearts have not grown old;
Passion or conquest, wander where they will,
Attend upon them still.

But now they drift on the still water,
Mysterious, beautiful;
Among what rushes will they build,
By what lake's edge or pool
Delight men's eyes when I awake some day
To find they have flown away?

The Kestrel

I caught this morning morning's minion, kingdom
  Of daylight's dauphin, dapple-dawn-dawn-drawn Falcon,
    in his riding
  Of the rolling level underneath him steady air, and
    striding
High there, how he rung upon the rein of a wimpling
    wing
In his ecstasy! then off, off forth on swing,
  As a skate's heel sweeps smooth on a bow-bend: the
    hurl and gliding
  Rebuffed the big wind. My heart in hiding
Stirred for a bird, – the achieve of, the mastery of
    the thing!

Gerard Manley Hopkins (1844–1889)

If there is one bird more than another that has hooked tens of thousands of British motorists on birdwatching, then it is the kestrel, that monarch of the motorways. I hope he hasn't caused too many accidents, because it takes quite an effort of will not to keep one's eyes fixedly upon him, as the wind-hover rides: 'the rolling level underneath him steady air.'

With good reason was he chosen in 1965 as the emblem of the Young Ornithologists' Club, the junior branch of the RSPB. It is one of the pleasanter side-effects of Britain's thousands of miles of motorways that the verges and central areas provide a valuable, undisturbed living-space for countless small rodents and birds. The kestrel was quick to discover this new food supply and with his conspicuous yet meticulous method of hunting won a whole new public. Among his admirers was a YOC member, John Savage, who was only fourteen when he wrote these nicely observed lines:

> Over the peaceful meadow is a kestrel,
> Like a kite, hovering, dropping, moving forward,
> Pulled by a thread of hunger,
> Yet unhurried.
>
> Searching the grass for a meal,
> An ever-watchful eye supported on vibrating wings;
> No movement evades it,
> Elegant but deadly.
>
> Not daring to move, every creature below freezes
> Under the cold fear of death.
> There is stillness for a few seconds ...
> Then a nerve breaks.
>
> An air-to-ground missile armed with a deadly war-head,
> A neat hole punched in the skull
> And a kestrel flies off with its prey.
> Peace returns to the meadow once more.

The YOC, inspired by young John's verses, carried out a survey to find out the number of kestrels hunting along Britain's motorways. The M6 came top of the list with an average of two sightings per mile. The estimate for the total kestrel population of the British Isles has been put at around 150,000 which probably exceeds all the other birds of prey put together. What is the reason for its success? In one word, adaptability. The kestrel's favourite diet of small rodents can be found even in an industrial wasteland and over the years it has learnt that shipyards, factories, and railway sidings can make attractive hunting grounds.

At the turn of the century, although it was the commonest bird of prey to be seen in London, there were no records of its having nested there. Then, in the thirties, it began nesting regularly on high places in central London, not excepting Nelson's Column. In these wholly urban settings the kestrel has adapted to live mainly on sparrows and the occasional pigeon, taken usually on the ground.

The explanation of the bird's move to the cities may be due in part to overcrowded conditions for it in the countryside. By the thirties, gamekeepers were at last beginning to realise the value of the kestrel as a destroyer of rodents and insects and often spared it the fate meted out to other hook-nosed birds. It was then that its numbers increased and the more adaptable of the birds began to spread out into the towns. The movement was intensified when the use of agricultural pesticides proved so deadly to hawks in rural areas. So it was that the gifted wildlife artist James Alder, the Newcastle birdman, was able to write to his local newspaper, the *Evening Chronicle* in the mid-sixties to tell of a kestrel's nest high up on a huge tower crane in a famous shipyard:

The nest was situated on a girder under the machine room on the swinging boom of the crane with a sheer drop of approximately 140 feet to the ground. Originally this nest had been built by a pair of rooks, and indeed the rooks had laid their complement of eggs when the kestrels, after a tussle, took over. When I first saw it the nest contained six red-brown kestrel eggs and one green speckled rook's. I had hoped to photograph this unusual clutch but when I returned with my camera, the hen kestrel had destroyed the last rook's egg. The rooks, it seems, having decided to nest in a shipyard had made up their minds to compete with the human builders below for engineering honours. They built their nest almost entirely of wire. The hen kestrel was sitting her eggs fairly tightly and it was possible to walk along the catwalk within eight feet of her before she left her nest, when she would fly around the crane and swoop at me to scare me away. Normally when I am birdwatching I am more used to the sighing of the wind through heather and the plaintive cries of moorland birds and I found the grinding crash of the huge gears in the machine room behind me almost unbearable; but the kestrel brooded her eggs unconcernedly. The great crane lifted tons of prefabricated sections, swung slowly and dropped them into position. The great hulk of the ship below acquired a set of ribs and a prow. But the kestrel thought nothing of these marvels. She had eggs to hatch.

And James watched them hatch and the nestlings grow strong until there came the day of the first solo flight:

I saw the first youngster launch himself into the vastness below him. He dropped and teetered on the air uncertainly and then, triumphantly, his

winnowing wings and frantic ruddering won him control and he was flying – to circle the crane and land on the platform near me.

One of the youngsters boobed his first flight and landed in a pool of bilge oil but James cleaned him up, trained him to hunt and as soon as he was able, released him to the wild.

I remember sharing the stage with James Alder at the Newcastle City Hall on 5 November 1970. On that occasion, the *Newcastle Evening Chronicle* billed us as, 'Alder and Dougall, double-act counter attraction to the pyromaniac pleasures of Guy Fawkes Night.'

James had with him a young kestrel which had been found injured and he had patiently nursed back to health. It had become so tame that he could do anything with it. He brought it onto the stage, released it and off it flew to perch on a beam high up at the back of the huge auditorium. At a call from James, down it swooped at once to perch on his shoulder. The bird seemed completely impervious to the bright lights and the crowded theatre. His trust was total and certainly not misplaced because, being a man of infinite patience, James painstakingly trained the bird to hunt for itself in the months to come and successfully returned it to the wild.

Perhaps one of the kestrel's most important assets in adapting to city life has been its astonishing manoeuvrability and mastery of flight. In a crowded scene it can hover and descend to snatch its prey from a small open space among buildings with a precision that a helicopter might envy.

And what a marvel it is to watch a kestrel riding out a gale on a day when no other bird would take to the air. It almost seems to relish the challenge. Sometimes it will hover for as long as a minute or more over one spot. In order to do this against a gusting wind and retain a fixed position it has frequently to adjust its speed of flight with miraculously quick reflexes. I am convinced too that kestrels in rough weather will sometimes fly for the sheer joy of it. E. L. Roberts had no doubts:

The memory of a wild day on the savage coast of Scotland comes to mind. A fierce autumn gale had lashed the sea to fury, shrieking through the sea-caves and howling fiendishly around the stacks and precipices. Flying spume eddied and swirled up to the cliff-tops where the wind whipped it away in great gobs across the fields. So violent was the wind that it almost took the breath; my ears were full of its tremendous roaring, and the gulls were tossed about like white rags in the turbulent air.

A male kestrel hung in the terrific, blasting upcurrent of air at the cliff-top, hovering without a single beat of the wings. His only movements were the alternate spread and contraction of tail and wing-feathers to preserve balance. The bird could scarcely have been hunting, for there was naught below but the raging surf. Clearly he was floating, effortlessly, in the fierce updraught for no other reason than sheer pleasure. And as I watched, the little falcon cried out, it seemed to me, for sheer joy and exuberance, his shrill 'quee-quee-quee-quee-quee' hurled away across the cliff-tops by the wild wind.

E. L. Roberts: 'The Happy Countryman'

Quite apart from his flying prowess, a male kestrel is a joy to behold. Admire his trim shape when perched on a solitary post in pale sunlight. The head and long tail shine silver-blue and there is a distinctive black band at the end of the tail. His face has black moustache-like stripes which gave him a raffish air and his back is cinnamon-red spotted with black. It takes the male three years to acquire this fine colouring. The immature birds resemble the female who is mostly brown with barring on the back and tail and heavy streaking on the underparts.

When in Suffolk I never tire of watching them hunting over the dunes, and they are equally plentiful in Hampstead too, where the Heath provides them with an ample supply of voles. For two years, in 1972 and 1973, a pair nested in a tall lime tree about fifty yards from the bedroom window of our Hampstead cottage. The third year they returned and were settling in nicely when the owners of another tiny cottage right at the foot of the tree decided urgent repairs were required to their roof. The kestrels stuck it out for ten days but the constant bashing and hammering below proved too much for them: they left and sadly have never returned. But for those two years they provided us with tremendous interest. The nest was high up in the fork of the tree and seemed a very rudimentary affair with a few sticks and twigs. There was no means of checking the number of eggs but, usually, four and sometimes as many as six eggs are laid and incubation takes about twenty-eight days. The female appeared to do all the sitting while the tiercel kept her well supplied with food.

161

Once the chicks had hatched, there was tremendous activity and considerable noise from dawn onwards. It was about a month before the young made their first tentative flights and at this time the female joined in the hunting too. Both parents continued to feed the young for two or three weeks after they had flown. The noise and excitement were such that I believe some of our neighbours were not altogether sorry when they departed. My only regret was that I hadn't had the time to make a more detailed study.

Since the very earliest times man has had a special relationship with the birds of prey, a kind of love-hate. The pursuit of falconry probably spread to Europe from the Middle East and the Bosphorus about 500 B.C. at the time of the Persian Invasions. One of the finest and most authoritative books on the sport is still *On the Art of Hunting with Birds* written by Emperor Frederick II of Germany in the thirteenth century.

Perhaps partly because of this ancient association there can be few sadder sights to come upon than a hawk crippled in the wing. The angler-poet, Herbert Palmer, was greatly affected by one he found that had been shot by a gamekeeper. It was spread wide and struggling on the grass:

> Such anguish filled each great round eye
> It wrung my heart and rocked my brain
> I longed for powers within the Sky
> To give it strength to fly again –
>
> To soar and swoop and hunt and prey,
> Fulfil its nature to the core;
> The sunlight seemed to leave the day;
> Upon my joy there closed a door.
>
> It glared at me in fear and pain,
> Then beat its wings and strove to fly.
> I stopped awhile, but could not aid;
> Then thought, as I went slowly by –
>
> We're pages from the self-same book;
> But you – you're done. I wait for God's wish.
> One hunts with beak, and one with hook,
> And one with word – birds, knaves, fools, fish.

The Kestrel

Above all, there is an uncompromising, arrogant timelessness about a hawk. Ted Hughes captures the spirit of it perfectly:

> I sit in the top of the wood, my eyes closed.
> Inaction, no falsifying dream
> Between my hooked head and hooked feet:
> Or in sleep rehearse perfect kills and eat.
>
> The convenience of the high trees!
> The air's buoyancy and the sun's ray
> Are of advantage to me;
> And the earth's face upward for my inspection.
>
> My feet are locked upon the rough bark.
> It took the whole of Creation
> To produce my foot, my each feather:
> Now I hold Creation in my foot
>
> Or fly up, and revolve it all slowly –
> I kill where I please because it is all mine.
> There is no sophistry in my body:
> My manners are tearing off heads –
>
> The allotment of death.
> For the one path of my flight is direct
> Through the bones of the living.
> No arguments assert my right:
>
> The sun is behind me.
> Nothing has changed since I began.
> My eye has permitted no change.
> I am going to keep things like this.

Ted Hughes (1930–   ): 'Hawk Roosting'

12

The Heron

Ye fisher herons watching eels
Robert Burns (1759–1796): 'Elegy'

For me, the lone grey heron standing sentinel-like in the shallows
embodies the very spirit of the marshland and the reed-beds, which
stretch away like a second sea behind the shingly coastline of north
Suffolk. The solitude, his statuesque patience, the pearl-grey landscape all invest the scene with a sense of poetic timelessness and
yet, for some reason, the heron has been little celebrated in
literature.

In the Middle Ages, the heyday of falconry, the bird's breeding
places were carefully protected for it was much prized as the quarry
of falcons. Tremendous contests took place in the skies. Some
accounts say that as the hawk stooped from above, the heron would
strike upwards with his dagger-like bill and even succeed in
impaling his persecutor. On the other hand Frank Lower an
authority on the bird, wrote in 1954: 'The heron's formidable bill
does not seem to have provided any protection during flight, but on
the ground it is a dangerous weapon, and more than a few falcons,
slow at "making-in" were badly stabbed.'

An unusual and highly disconcerting defence mechanism on the
part of the heron was hinted at by the sixteenth-century ornithologist
Turner, who claimed that the bird 'routs Eagles and Hawks, if they
attack it suddenly, by very liquid mutings of the belly, and thereby
defends itself.' Anyway it is clear that although a cold-blooded killer
by the stream, the heron often met his own fate from those terrible
talons in the sky:

The Heron

Stock-still upon that stone from day to day
I see thee watch the river for thy prey.
– Yes, I'm the tyrant here; but when I rise
The well-trained falcon braves me in the skies.
Then comes the tug of war, of strength and skill,
He dies impaled on my up-darted bill;
Or powerless in his grasp, my doom I meet,
Dropt as a trophy at his master's feet.

James Montgomery (1771–1854): 'Birds'

Perhaps the luckless heron would then, in his turn, be impaled –
on a spit – for he was highly esteemed as good eating and the
nestlings in particular were thought a delicacy. At one time no royal
banquet failed to have heron on the menu and even as recently as
1812 six birds were among the roasts at a feast in the Hall of the
Stationers Company in the City of London.

Today, we prize him just for himself and no doubt many a
holiday-maker has been aroused to take an interest in birdlife by the
sight of that still, grey figure on the bank. After all, the heron is one
of the largest and most impressive looking birds in Europe with a
wing span of about five feet and yet, surprisingly, only turning the
scales at four pounds or less.

His flight may appear slow and ponderous but is much faster than
it looks: a heron can fly at thirty-miles-an-hour for long distances.
The head and long neck are kept well tucked in, the wings arched,
and the legs, trailing behind for five inches or so, help to give him
balance and direction:

The heron, with discordant notice, rose,
And flapping wings upon the cloudy air;
Then pois'd awhile, its plumaged rudder set
This way or that.

Phil Robinson: 'Hermitage' from 'The Poet's Birds'

On the ground he is a sober-looking bird in his plumage of grey
and white streaked with black and the long dark crest gives him a
look of refined distinction. The yellow pickaxe bill has slight
serrations on both mandibles; the prey, once grabbed, is in a vice.
His stilt-like legs are ideal for wading and the unwebbed feet are

huge, the long spidery toes preventing him from sinking in soft mud. The female looks very similar but her colouring is duller and the crest shorter: in appearance, at least, she is less striking.

For some reason, the eighteenth-century French naturalist, Comte de Buffon was most ungallant in his summing up of the heron, as he growled:

But how various soever the heron kind may be in their colours or bills they all have but one characteristic of cowardice and rapacity, indolence, yet immoderate hunger. Other birds grow fat by an abundant supply of food; but these, though destructive and voracious, have always lean and carrion bodies, as if plenty were not sufficient for their support.

Can it be that Buffon himself was an indifferent angler? Perhaps he lacked patience, a virtue of which Old Franky, as the heron is sometimes called in Norfolk, has an abundant supply. This affectionate nickname comes of course from the bird's harsh cry, sounding something like 'frank, frank'. The ancient name of the heron was hern, heronshaw or hernshaw which derive from the old French heronceau. Spenser uses it in these lines from *The Faerie Queene* VI. VII. 9:

> As when a cast of Faulcons make their flight
> At an Hernshaw that lyes aloft on wing.

Anglers so marvelled at the heron's successful fishing technique that for hundreds of years they managed to convince themselves that his feet and legs exuded a special oil which fish found irresistible. At one time they used to smear their bait with heron fat and I have heard that even today on the Faroes the bird's foot is sometimes carried for luck.

Another widely held idea was that the bird, when hunting in the shallows, would shake a fine grey powder out of his plumage and that this substance lying on the surface would entice the curious fish to their doom.

Anglers evidently found it hard to believe that apart from his astonishing eyesight, long neck and legs and deadly bill his only secret weapon was endless patience. In any case, the heron is not quite such a menace as some might suppose. He will eat almost

anything. Apart from fish, he takes crabs, prawns, frogs, mice, small birds, grasshoppers, waterbeetles and, in hard weather, will think nothing of adding coot, moorhen, duck or the occasional rat to his long menu even if it chokes him.

In *Oddities of Natural History* Eric Parker mentions such a case. A correspondent signing himself M.A. wrote from Scotland on 13 December 1910:

I was stalking up a burn, where duck was sometimes to be found, when on turning a corner I came on a heron, not five yards from me, with a water-hen in its beak, trying to swallow it. It choked and choked, but evidently found it too big a morsel, and could not get it down. Suddenly aware of my presence it disgorged the moorhen and flew away. The moorhen also immediately scuttled away into the rushes, apparently none the worse for its adventure.

I have also heard of several instances where a heron has been seen to take a weasel. Eric Parker cites a case when a Mr C. C. Tyrrell Giles of Hopton, Thetford on 9 December 1911 sent for examination a bird which had been choked through trying to swallow a dabchick. These were the conclusions:

From the position in which the grebe was lodged it is evident that it was approaching the heron, and was seized by the head and neck, which were swallowed, when the extension of its wings prevented further passage into the gullet, and both birds were suffocated. The heron was a fine bird with the following measurements: Total length from tip of beak to end of tail, 40 in.; beak from forehead, 5 in.; wing from carpal joint, 18 in.; tarsus 6½ in.; bare part of tibia, 2½ in.; expanse of wing, 5½ feet. We do not remember to have met with another instance of a heron attempting to swallow so large a victim as an adult little grebe.

Mr Giles had obviously not heard of the onslaught on the moorhen. But these are of course exceptional cases and those herons must have been driven to desperate measures by very severe weather.

When conditions are normal the favourite food is eels. Eels are distinctly uncooperative and, once grabbed, thresh about like mad often entwining themselves round the heron's neck in desperate attempts to avoid the inevitable. In the process, which often lasts several minutes, the bird's plumage can become covered in slime.

When cleaning up afterwards, a heron coats its feathers with a substance called 'powder down' which is secreted in special glands on the sides of the breast, above the tail and elsewhere. This reduces the stickiness, which is then finally groomed away with the help of a comb, positioned for the purpose on the claw of the third, long toe.

It mustn't be thought that herons are only to be seen in remote, solitary places. Certainly in Henry VIII's time they cannot have been a great rarity in and around London. He was concerned that they might be poached and issued a proclamation to preserve them: 'from his Palace at Westminster to St Giles-in-the-Fields and from thence to Islington, Hampstead, Highgate and Hornsey Park'. At this time falconry was still a royal sport and Henry had need of the herons. Incidentally, the royal falcons had been kept in the mews at Charing Cross since Richard II's time. Henry then decided to keep his horses there and so the word 'mews' took on a new meaning. Today in London herons can still be seen.

In the mid-sixties I often used to exercise my two dogs in Regents Park. One cold, still, February morning – standing hunched and dejected among the boats by the pool, was the solitary outline of Old Franky. It surprised me a little at the time and I assumed that he was a straggler from a colony established since 1914 on an island at Walthamstow reservoir to the north of London. There among dense thickets of elder and hawthorn stood sycamores, willows and a number of mature hawthorn trees about thirty feet high. I knew that some trees held three or four nests which led to overcrowding, so I guessed this character might be on the look-out for new quarters. There was not much doubt: a small wild heronry was in fact set up on one of the islands in the park in 1968. The only people who were less than delighted were nearby residents who had been increasingly mystified by the disappearance of goldfish from their garden ponds. One man I knew finally solved the problem by placing a stone heron in his pool, which successfully kept the live marauders at bay.

It seems clear that herons, like kestrels and also many members of the crow family are finding that there is less persecution and a good living to be had in town. If it were not for the crows and rooks which mob them unmercifully, I feel sure that far more herons would take up residence in our city parks and certainly on Hampstead Heath in London. Many a time have I seen a grey fisher standing wistfully by the ponds there, but I fear the all too numerous crows will never allow him to nest.

Probably more is known about the size of the population of herons in England and Wales than of any wild bird in the world. This is because for nearly fifty years there have been annual counts organised by the British Trust for Ornithology. These show that the numbers have varied very little and fluctuate at around 5,000 pairs. The most important factor is the weather and after severe winters it takes a few years for the population figures to recover.

The rate of recovery after the terrible freeze-up of 1963, which reduced their numbers to just over 2,000 pairs, was exceptionally slow. This may have been due to the widespread use in the sixties of deadly agricultural pesticides and chemicals. Now that more control is exercised over their use, and waters are in general somewhat less polluted, the outlook for the heron is brighter.

At the time of writing, their numbers are at a peak and probably exceed 5,000 pairs. Perhaps due to overcrowding, scattered pairs are now breeding outside the traditional colonies. The usual pattern is that the birds disperse in the winter and become solitary hunters. Towards the end of January they return to their ancestral homes and the breeding cycle begins.

Most heronries are in woodland close to water and in many cases the birds return to the same nests year after year. These are built of sticks and are often perched precariously at the tops of the tallest trees. Nest building is usually just a repair job and carried out by both sexes. For such exceptionally ungainly birds they contrive to manoeuvre about in the treetops with the daredevil skill of high-wire artists. There is certainly no truth in the quaint idea that herons build a nest with two holes in it so that they can sit with their legs dangling down.

The male bird does most of the stick collecting and there is a charming little ceremony as he returns to the nest. On approaching, he usually gives a few loud croaks, straightens himself out, alights, raises his crest and proudly proffers his gift. Heads are thrown back in joyous greeting and the bills of both sexes now show a distinctly rosy flush. A few days after mating, the first pale-greenish-blue egg

Plates: 5 **Kestrel** 6 **Heron**
7 **Avocet** 8 **Osprey**

5

is laid followed by one every two days. The clutch usually varies from three to five and once the first egg is laid the bills revert to their usual yellow colour. If for any reason the eggs are lost, the bills again become pinkish and the birds display and mate again before producing a new clutch.

Incubation, which lasts about twenty-eight days, starts before the clutch is completed and so the eggs hatch out at intervals and the young vary considerably in size. In consequence, if food is at all scarce the younger and weaker nestlings stand no chance. This method ensures that, in hard times, the largest of the young at least will get enough food to build up strength to leave the nest. It is survival of the fittest. And woe betide any nestling which strays from the parental home or falls to the ground as the parent will bring food only to the nest itself.

During the first ten days, the young are helpless and one adult must be on constant guard against marauding crows and jackdaws. Meantime the other parent may have to fly considerable distances in search of food. With the increase of intensive farming methods, ditches in many places are being replaced by piped drains and the countryside becomes ever tidier. For a heron this means a diminishing supply of prey.

After one of these foraging expeditions which may last up to six or seven hours, the return to the nest can be spectacular in the extreme. I like Jim Flegg's description in *Country Life* of 1 May 1975:

Birds on their return journey come in over the heronry at a great height and with no means of making a steady descent to the colony. They seem to delight in 'whiffling' in a breath-taking aerobatic display as they tumble helter skelter out of the sky, twisting from side to side in a series of tight spirals and half-turns.

The noise is indescribable as the young rush at their parent, pecking at its bill to make it disgorge its cropful of prey onto the floor of the nest. Then a battle royal begins over the regurgitated mess of frogs, eels, small rodents, fish or perhaps waterbird chicks. It has been estimated that in the two months' nesting period something like 230 lbs of varied food are brought to the treetop home.

W. H. Hudson wrote about a visit to one of his favourite heronries in a small wood near the Norfolk Broads:

On the occasion of my last visit this heronry was in the most interesting stage, when the young birds were fully grown and were to be seen standing up on their big nests or on the topmost branches of the trees waiting to be fed. At some spots in the wood where the trees stand well apart I could count as many as forty to fifty young birds standing in this way, in families of two, three, and four. It was a fine sight, and the noise they made at intervals was a fine thing to hear. The heron is a bird with a big voice.

He then describes the scene as the returning parent approaches the heronry on widespread wings which appeared dark-blue against the shining light of the sky:

All the young birds, stretched up to their full height, would watch its approach, and each and every one of them would regard the returning bird as its too-long absent parent with food to appease its own furious hunger; and as it came swooping over the colony there would be a tremendous storm of wild expectant cries – strange cat- and dog-like growling, barking, yelping, whining, screaming; and this would last until the newcomer would drop upon its own tree and feed its own young, whereupon the tempest would slowly subside, only to be renewed on the appearance of the next great blue bird coming down over the wood.

By midsummer the gawky youngsters will have fledged and very different they look from their parents with pale-grey and reddish-brown as the main colours and they lack the long crest. The squads of trainees have much to learn in the art of stalking and hunting in the shallows as Alfred Rees memorably describes in *The Heron of Castle Creek*:

The young herons were undoubtedly filled with the importance of their early lessons in obtaining food, and were closely attentive to every motion on the part of their mother. When she advanced, they all advanced, when she trod, they all trod, lifting their long shanks with nervous clumsiness. Generally they moved in single file behind the parent bird, but sometimes, as with excessive caution she stalked a trout or a minnow that had darted to refuge beneath a pebble in the shallows, or a mouse, or a frog, or a

beetle that had hidden in the grass on the bank of the lake, they quietly
stole up in line beside her the better to enjoy the sight of good hunting.
Hardly had the mother lifted her head after striking her prey, when the
young birds, crowding around her, and feebly flapping their wings, begged
with low, harsh cries for food. If the catch proved to be an insignificant

item in her usual bill of fare, the mother heron swallowed it with ludicrous haste, but if she caught a frog or a trout of any considerable size she at once doubled back among her excited brood, so that the water she had not already fished might remain undisturbed; then, pretending to find difficulty in eluding their pursuit, she hastened haphazard hither and thither till her most vigorous pursuer forced her to surrender the prize. The excitement having abated, she resumed her stalking; and the members of her awkward squad formed again in line to the rear.

In 1971, at the RSPB's famous Minsmere Reserve, the Senior Warden, Herbert Axell, was able to register yet another 'first' for the Reserve when a pair of herons nested and fledged young from a nest in the reeds. This may have been due to overcrowding in the adjoining treetop colony and the next year another pair followed the example. There is I believe only one other place in England where herons will nest on the ground, although in Scotland and in Holland it is not quite so uncommon. It was certainly a tribute to Herbert that the shy birds felt secure enough to take their chance at ground level.

Perhaps my most vivid memory of nesting herons is of the great mixed colonies in the ancient cork oaks of the Coto Doñana National Park in south-western Spain. Here, stately storks occupy the crowns of the trees, leaving the higher outside branches to the herons. Snowy-white spoonbills seem to roost everywhere, their plumage and droppings transforming the huge twisted trees into weird white mansions. The shy squacco herons take the interior branches and the graceful cattle egrets frequent the lower boughs. In the teeming wilderness of the Coto predators abound and the birds have evidently learnt that communal nesting can give them a greater measure of security.

It is an unforgettable sight when, as the sun goes down, the nests and the outlines of hundreds of roosting birds are silhouetted against a golden glow:

> The creatures sit, in drowsy rows,
> With their plumage doubly bright
> Slumbering in the golden light.
>
> *Phil Robinson: 'Rothay' from 'The Poet's Birds'*

13

The Osprey

On a gaunt and shattered tree
By the black cliffs of obsidian
I saw the nest of the osprey.
Nothing remained of the tree
For this lonely eyrie
Save the undaunted bole
That cycles of wind had assaulted
And, clinging still to the bole,
Tenacious the topmost branches.
Here, to scan all the heavens,
Nested the osprey.

Jessie B. Rittenhouse: from 'A Bird-Lover's Anthology'

The return, phoenix-like, of the spectacular chocolate and white fish-hawk to nest, after an absence of fifty years, by a loch side in Scotland fired the imagination of the British public in a quite remarkable way. It was in the spring of 1959 that three young were reared successfully in an eyrie at the top of a tall Scots pine at Loch Garten on Speyside. The circumstances were dramatic and the event a triumph of imaginative nature conservation for the RSPB.

Only the previous year, with high hopes, a continuous day and night watch had been kept at an eyrie built at the top of a low tree beside the same loch, near Nethybridge. It was a hurriedly improvised operation throwing a considerable strain on the four or five people involved. The birds began sitting near the end of the second week in May, so there was a five weeks' uncomfortable vigil ahead.

On the night of 3 June it was the turn of Philip Brown, a former

RSPB head, to be on watch in the makeshift hessian hide two hundred yards from the tree. At two thirty in the morning, in the half light, he suddenly realised that one of the lower boughs was shaking. He alerted RSPB Senior Warden, Herbert Axell, and they both rushed to investigate. As he wrote afterwards:

It was one of the most desperate moments of my life. The ospreys' nest was not more than twenty-five feet from the ground and the tree extremely simple to climb. We had nearly two hundred yards to run over an extremely wet bog in our attempt to catch the intruder. I remember only too well how my boots sank into the ground. As one tried to pull them out it was as if some devil were trying to hold one down. However, I think we probably got within about fifty yards of the tree when the chap spotted us and got out very quickly. He was able to drop out of the tree onto the soft ground without any fear of harming himself, though he left a pretty deep footmark to show where he landed. He was younger than either of us and we think that he probably wore light shoes; at any rate he got away into thick cover in the half light and completely eluded us.

Philip Brown: 'Birds of Prey'

They found two smashed eggs at the foot of the tree.

As a result of that disaster, nothing was left to chance in 1959; near-military methods were used in 'Operation Osprey' to ensure security for the birds. The foot of the tree was fortified with a tangle of barbed wire and an electronic device attached to the trunk. This was designed to ring a buzzer in the watchers' hide if contact were made. A look-out post was then set up for the public and, in no time, people were rolling up in their thousands to this fairly remote spot in the Highlands, a few miles north of the Cairngorms. The precautions paid off; three young were raised and since that spring of 1959 more than half a million people have made the trek to Loch Garten. In all, over thirty young ospreys have flown from the site and now, nearly twenty years later, they have spread out and there are probably as many as fourteen secret eyries elsewhere in Scotland.

In the process, the osprey has surely become one of the most observed birds in the world. Television has seen to that. Throughout the sixties and for the first few years of the seventies, when I was involved with BBC Television News, the osprey story became a hardy annual and probably did more than any other event to publicise the invaluable conservation work carried out by the RSPB. To crown it all, as a result of the 'Save a Place for Birds' Appeal, which I had the honour of launching with Lord Home as President of the Appeal Committee, the Society was able in 1975 to purchase the nest site at Loch Garten with fifteen hundred acres of forest, loch and moorland to make a magnificent Reserve for all time. It was a classic item of good news when there was precious little of it to be found. And yet, even this story had its set-backs: in some years gales, in others egg-collectors took their toll.

As recently as May 1977 BBC Television's Nine O'Clock News splashed a story, between the doings of President Carter and the Reverend Ian Paisley, to the effect that a clutch of four osprey eggs had been stolen from a secret site in the Highlands.

Obviously it's not possible to mount a twenty-four hour watch at all the sites – it now takes over a hundred volunteers and four fully paid staff at the Loch Garten eyrie alone. So, some warped individual was able to prevent the hatching of the only clutch of four osprey eggs to be laid in Britain this century – the normal number being two or three. It is some comfort perhaps to know that the maximum fine for egg stealing under the Protection of Birds Act has recently been raised to £500.

There can be few more persecuted birds in history. At one time, the osprey was a quite common visitor to large estuaries all around our coasts, especially in the autumn, when there were many young birds to be seen. In 1838 a pair were even reported to have nested in Devonshire, on Lundy Island, and in 1847 another pair attempted to nest at Monksilver in west Somerset but were shot by a gamekeeper. It was a combination of the ruthlessness of keepers, the hostility of anglers, the depredations of egg-collectors and the widespread habit, even among naturalists, of shooting any unfamiliar bird they saw that, in the last century, finally proved too much for the osprey.

One of the most notorious nest-robbers was a professional egg-collector by the name of Lewis Dunbar. Here he describes one of his many exploits – a raid in 1848 on a traditional nesting site. It was an eyrie perched on the south-west tower of a ruined castle at Loch an Eilein in the forest of Rothiemurchus. And he walked twenty miles to get there:

On a bright April day I walked from Grantown to the loch, swam in and explored the old castle, getting my bare legs stung by nettles, and finding the best and easiest way of climbing to the nest. I climbed up and secured three eggs, put them in my bonnet, placed the latter on my head, and took to the water again. On reaching the shore, a woman at the gamekeeper's house saw me and fled quickly inside.

Dunbar and other notorious collectors made numerous raids in subsequent years and they didn't stop at taking the eggs, but in many cases shot the adult birds as well. It was in 1852 that he came to make his fifth onslaught on the ill-fated eyrie at Loch an Eilein and afterwards sent the eggs to the naturalist John Wolley. He then wrote this graphic account which appeared in 'Ootheca Wolleyana':

The three eggs I took myself on the night of 8th May 1852, between eleven and twelve o'clock. As it was very dark and no moon, I had the precaution to take my cousin along with me, and he proved of great service. I took off my clothes and put on my life-preserver, attaching a cord to the back of it. By the help of a fusee I was able to distinguish that the time I was able to launch my carcase into the water was twenty-five minutes to twelve. I got over quite safe. The cock bird flew away before I reached the island; and after I had climbed up to the top of the ruin, and was just at the nest, I put out my hand to catch the hen, but when she felt me she gave a loud scream and flew away also. On arriving at the island I had fixed the cord to a bush; and on coming back I had some difficulty in finding it owing to the darkness of the night; but when I did so, I secured it to my belt and bawled to my cousin to pull, which he did. In the middle I was taken with cramp, but he succeeded in hauling me out. After dressing, we forded the river which was very high at the time; and on going across with my cousin on my back, I stumbled, and down he went, but he managed to get to his feet and this put an end to our adventures.

With characters like that around, the ospreys hadn't a chance, although they were at least spared the attentions of Dunbar when he emigrated to Australia, no doubt in search of even wider scope for his talents.

Many birds of all kinds were also greatly persecuted during the first twenty years of this century for the plumage trade. One of the worst sufferers was the graceful little egret. In the marshes of southern Spain and elsewhere the birds were sacrificed to women's

fashion. The elegant plumes coveted by the millinery trade were often torn from the living birds at the time when they were at their most splendid in the spring. The English milliners called this plume of feathers on a hat an 'osprey'. They probably meant to call them 'a spray' but the bird's name confused them and so 'osprey plumes' they became. This, at least, was one fate the fish-hawk did not have to suffer and, in any case, the miserable trade came to an end in 1921, when, thanks mainly to the RSPB, it was made illegal to import the plumes into Britain.

In the sixteenth century however the osprey had been subjected to another kind of heartless exploitation. It was mentioned by William Harrison writing in 1577:

We have also ospraies, which breed with us in parks and woods, whereby the keepers of the same do reap in breeding time no small commodity: for so soon almost as the young are hatched, they tie them to the butt ends or ground ends of sundry trees, where the old ones finding them, do never cease to bring fish unto them, which the keepers take and eat from them, and commonly is such as is well fed, or not of the worst sort.

There is no question of the bird's prowess as a fisherman. I like E. L. Roberts' description of one he was lucky enough to see over Hickling Broad in Norfolk in 1956:

Followed by a screaming mob of black-headed gulls, the osprey was flapping steadily towards us at a height of about seventy feet. As I watched, fascinated, the bird wheeled suddenly with tail spread like a fan, then checked and plunged headlong into the broad with a mighty splash. He was up again in a split second, momentarily enveloped in a shimmering cloud of flying spray – the 'shake' that always follows the fish-hawk's plunge. And in his talons was clutched head foremost, a one-and-a-half-pound bream. Never have I seen anything more spectacular.

E. L. Roberts: 'The Happy Countryman'

Michael Drayton, the Warwickshire poet, who lived from 1561 to 1631 implied that fish knew they hadn't a chance once the bird hovered above them:

The Osprey, oft here seen, though seldom here it breeds,
Which over them the fish no sooner do espy,

But (betwixt him and them, by an antipathy)
Turning their bellies up, as though their death they saw,
They at his pleasure lie, to stuff his glutt'nous maw.

Drayton was probably referring there to pike, a fish which likes to bask near the surface of the water.

After catching its prey by plunging feet first, the osprey usually carries it to a tree and holding the fish securely in its huge talons tears strips off the flesh with its deeply hooked bill. The scaly feet have spines so that the fish is easier to grab and carry.

If his fishing is spectacular, then the courtship display is doubly so. After wintering in Africa, the male is usually the first to arrive at the eyrie site; at Loch Garten the average date is 3rd April. This is when he is at his most splendid: a creamy-white head distinguished by a dark-brown band across the face giving him a raffish, buccaneering look. His breast is an immaculate white shield with gingery-brown markings at the throat. The sickle-like bill and talons are black, the legs pale-blue. His back is a chocolate-brown cloak and, full-spread, the wings will span five feet or more.

Given a clear, bright morning, he may circle round and then climb with rapid wing-beats up to as high as a thousand feet. For a moment, kestrel-like, he will hover tail outspread, then down he plummets in a breathtaking dive. With the arrival of the female a few days later, his display and continual high-pitched cries reach a peak of excitement. The hen watches admiringly, standing on the old eyrie. She is slightly larger and similarly marked, though less distinctive and with more brown in her plumage.

After mating, the serious business of building up the nest begins. The same one will be used year after year. Sticks of all sizes are gathered or broken from trees and the male carries the large ones in his talons, as he does a fish – pointing fore and aft. The eyrie is a big solid structure measuring at least four feet across; it has to be strong to stand up to gale-force winds. The nest-lining, of moss, heather, turf or bark is provided mainly by the female; then in about the third week of April the two or three eggs are usually laid, incubation starts and it will last on average for thirty-five days. This is mostly done by the hen, while the male's job is to go foraging for food. And a great deal of fishing he has to do, as the young will remain in the nest for seven or eight weeks.

My last visit to the ospreys in Scotland was on a memorable trip with a party of RSPB Council members in June 1972. Our first stop was at Dunkeld in Perthshire. That evening we drove out to a 240 acre Reserve set up by the Scottish Wildlife Trust a few years earlier, at the Loch of the Lowes. It is a smallish loch and in an exceptionally beautiful setting, as so much of Scotland must have looked before the forests were felled and the sheep came.

The Scottish lochs were scooped out by glaciers which sculpted this landscape so many thousands of years ago. No one knows for sure how this particular loch got its name, though it may well have derived from the fact that here hounds used to be unleashed or 'lowsed' for boar hunting.

That evening the waters of the loch were as smooth as silk as we filed quietly into the wooden observation hut. There, on the western shore, perched at the very top of a substantial pine we could clearly see the eyrie with the female and three young.

They could be safe there thanks to the voluntary helpers who had mounted a twenty-four hour watch until the eggs were hatched. On this occasion the young were being protected by the eagle eyes of a retired bank manager and a fresh-faced lad of fourteen with tow-coloured hair. They told us that pellets collected from below the nest showed perch to be the main food and not, as is more usual, the surface-basking pike.

The next day we headed for Loch Garten, driving through Glen Garry to Dalwhinnie on Loch Ericht, then by Glen Truim with the Cairngorms away on our right. At Kingussie we turned right for a visit to a new RSPB Reserve, Insh Fen, an excellent mixed and wetland area with many curlews, redshanks and snipe.

And so finally to Loch Garten, the famous site which has borne the brunt of the visitors. Here we saw a female with two young in the nest.

This is where, in 1959, it all started – one of the most uplifting wildlife stories of our generation. It is also a classic case of how controlled access can safely be allowed to shy and rare breeding birds.

Perhaps it has also reminded us of the truth of Emerson's words:

> We need the tonic of wildness –
> In wildness is the preservation of the world.

14

The Avocet

If 'Operation Osprey' was an undoubted triumph for the RSPB, then the return of the avocet was doubly so. The one needed near-military methods of security; the other involved three additional requirements: the right conditions for breeding, a plentiful food supply and an extraordinary degree of vigilance to ensure the birds' safety in bad weather and to guard the young from predators of all kinds.

Equally, if London milliners at the turn of the century confused a spray with an osprey, then in Britain today there are probably many people for whom the name avocet has little meaning. I even heard of a young schoolboy who a few years back got thoroughly mixed up after a trip to Minsmere. Right in front of the hide he had seen two avocets and a grey plover; but when asked to write about the visit he put them down as 'two haversacks and a grey pullover'. Obviously not a member of the Young Ornithologists' Club.

The name in fact derives from the Italian 'avosetta' which in turn comes from the Latin 'avis' a bird, and the diminutive Italian ending, rather than small size, suggests delicacy or elegance. But, in his time, the avocet has had many names. In the seventeenth century the Norfolk philosopher and naturalist Sir Thomas Browne wrote of the bird: 'Avoseta called shoohing-horne a tall black and white bird with a bill semi-circularly reclining or bowed upward so that it is not easy to conceive how it can feed . . . a summer marsh bird and not unfrequent in Marshland.'

Shoohing-horne was a name given because of the bird's most distinctive feature, the up-tilted bill with which it sweeps from side to side in the shallows when feeding; for the same reason the avocet was sometimes known as the Cobbler's-awl duck or simply Crooked-bill. Another name Scooper also referred to its manner of feeding and Yelper, rather unkindly, to its cry. This is a loud 'kleep kleep' when alarmed. The flight call is a musical 'kluut' which in fact is the name given to the bird by the Dutch.

Up to the beginning of the nineteenth century, these calls were a by no means uncommon sound, especially on the eastern and south-eastern coastal marshes and on estuaries south of the Humber. But then, even more than the drainage of wetlands for agriculture, it was the merciless greed of egg-collectors and the breech-loading gun that finally drove the bird from our shores.

The avocet's beauty may also have hastened its extinction, as it was greatly prized in a glass case for Victorian drawing rooms and the eggs were taken not only for collections but for eating as well. Henry Stevenson, the nineteenth-century Norfolk naturalist, described how avocets' eggs at Salthouse were gathered by scores to make puddings and pancakes, and the gunners actually unloaded their big guns at the birds in wanton sport.' One of his contemporaries, the Rev. Mr Lubbock, also refers to them: 'They used formerly to breed at Salthouse near Holt, but are now extinct there; they were much harassed, as their feathers are valuable to make artificial flies with.'

It seems the last avocets to breed successfully anywhere in Britain had been a pair on Romney Marsh in 1842. Thereafter, colonies continued to exist in Europe, given suitable conditions, and the nearest were across the North Sea in the remaining wild wetlands and among the polders of Holland.

Writing in 1927, the famous ornithologist T. A. Coward could not help making an unfavourable comparison:

The Dutch are proud of their birds, and know how to keep them. An unkind but not wholly untrue Dutch assertion was that they preserved their birds so that Englishmen might rob their nests. Dutch ornithologists have learnt a lesson, and Government as well as private restrictions are enforced.

[And he then describes the peaceful scene in Holland:]
The cultivated polder is not our ideal of a bird haunt, but we had not left the haven of Oudeschild many minutes before we saw graceful black and white avocets feeding in shallow pools beside the road. They waded un-

concerned, swinging their slender upturned bills from side to side like tiny
scythes, mowing insects or tiny crustaceans from the water. A passing car
caused no alarm; had we back-fired it is doubtful if they would have
associated the sound with gun-fire, for guns are unfamiliar.

T. A. Coward: 'Bird Life at Home and Abroad'

Curiously enough, twenty years later, by which time we had all
become familiar with gunfire, it was the changed conditions due to
war that brought the avocets back to the east coast. It must be the
most famous of all post-war bird stories and has been fully told by
the late Philip Brown of the RSPB in his *Avocets in England*. More
recently my good friend Herbert Axell has also told the avocet
story in his excellent book *Minsmere, Portrait of a Bird Reserve*.

Briefly, with the war, much of the Suffolk coastline was banned
to the public and low-lying grazing land and marshes were flooded
as a defence measure. When peace came and the sluices began
operating again at Minsmere, situated midway between Southwold
and Aldeburgh, ideal conditions had developed for wading birds.
Meantime, the avocets' breeding grounds in the Netherlands, a
hundred miles across the North Sea, had been denied to them
because of deep flooding and other war-time action. So, a few of the
birds evidently decided to try their luck again in England.

On 8 April 1947 four pairs of avocets were found to be breeding
at Minsmere and, later that summer, another four pairs were
discovered on Havergate Island near Orford, twelve miles to the
south. The RSPB which then had only 5,000 members and a tiny
headquarters in part of a building in London's Victoria Street,
moved fast and in 1948 the local landowner at Minsmere, Captain
Stuart Ogilvie, agreed to lease 1,500 acres to the Society as a bird
reserve. That same year, in spite of its limited finances, the RSPB
decided to take the plunge and purchase Havergate Island.

There was immense interest and excitement: not only had the
avocets returned to breed in England after more than a hundred
years, but many of our ornithologists had never set eyes on one
before. Among them was A. W. P. Robertson and his admiration
knew no bounds:

It was a remarkable occasion, and I cannot remember being more impressed on first acquaintance with a bird. Indeed the media of words and

pictures are most inadequate to convey the haunting beauty of the living avocet. It is black and white, of course, with long slate-blue legs, and a black upturned bill; these externals, moreover, are admirably put together, the legs being long enough to give it dignity, the pied plumage so designed as to be both simple and striking. And of that astonishing bill – well one can but say that in specimens and pictures it looks grotesque but in the living bird it simply could not be otherwise; the whole pattern is integrated and finished by the delicate upward curve. But these are no more than the shell – the bust and hip measurements, as it were, of the Venus de Milo. As the avocet walks, each foot is lifted almost to the horizontal before it is advanced and set down again with feline grace, and the balance and poise of the bird's movements are a ballerina's despair, exquisite in their perfection. In flight it has the purposeful quick beat of so many waders, and the pure white wings edged with ebony carry the body most nobly as it tapers into the long point of blue legs stretched beyond the tail.

... Few creatures that I know, except, perhaps, the first-rate, thoroughbred racehorse, have quite such an air of being a cut above the company they keep. The richly coloured sheld-duck and the neat black-headed gull look dumpy and coarse beside it, the neighbouring peewits cast from very common clay.

A. W. P. Robertson: 'Birds Wild and Free'

What greater inspiration could the Society have had and what better choice as an emblem?

Besides its exceptional elegance and other engaging attributes, the avocet also has the advantage for the birdwatcher of instant recognition. There is very little difference in appearance throughout the year and the sexes also look alike. In flight too there is no mistaking it: apart from the distinctive black and white markings and rapid wing-beats, it is highly proficient at climbing or changing direction and the wings are often slightly arched, rather like a butterfly. The avocet is a true waterbird: if, when feeding in the shallows, the water suddenly deepens it will carry straight on with no hesitation until it is swimming. Frequently it will up-end like a duck.

By mid-April considerable pre-nesting activity takes place. Small groups of birds are often seen chasing each other in single file over a spit of land and then taking wing to continue their chase. Occasionally, two will detach themselves, rising up several feet and sparring with their long and powerful legs. Meantime the females crouch submissively, heads and necks stretched over the water.

First attempts are made at scraping a shallow nest, pieces of dead grass are thrown about, there is much bobbing of heads and then, in a week or so, the pair-bonds are formed.

The mating is a charming ceremony. After much preening by both birds, the female crouches almost flat in the water with wings spread, while the cock edges nearer first from one side then the other. He then mounts her with wings almost vertical to keep his balance. After mating, the female rises, they cross bills and run forward a few paces, the male stretching one wing across her back, as though in affection.

In the dry sand the nest is just a scrape, but when sited on a muddy area it may be more substantial. Avocets, unlike coots or moorhens, are not very good at building up their nests in flood conditions and the warden will often have to do it for them. Both birds take part in incubation and the usual number of eggs is four.

After about twenty-three days the young hatch and within twelve hours are busily darting about, pecking at the ground and swimming with great assurance and surprising speed. They are a delight to see: four-inch-long bundles of greyish-brown feathers with whitish underneaths, the tiny bills only slightly turned up. Development is rapid and within a week they are moving their bills from side to side through the water in imitation of their parents.

This is the time of greatest danger and the adults have a frenzied time trying to keep their chicks from straying. Enemies abound and although the parents are valiant in defence, the young can so easily be snatched up by a heron, a kestrel, a gull or even a moorhen or coot. In spite of their elegant appearance, avocet parents at this time are full of nervous aggression. Their delicate bills are useless as weapons so they make use of their strong legs. When attacking on the ground they first give a kind of shoulder charge, then sometimes jump over their enemy, at the same time striking out with their legs. From the air they swoop down in a power dive and end with legs outstretched. On these occasions the bird can be a surprisingly formidable opponent.

After about six weeks, the surviving young are able to fly and parties form before moving away to the south. From ringing, it is known that some birds winter in the River Tamar in south Devon, others across the water in Brittany, yet others in Spain and Portugal.

The main winter quarters are the salt and alkaline lakes of East Africa.

It was in those heady post-war years of their return to breed in England that I first became acquainted with the Suffolk coast and, with a base in a cottage there, I have been privileged to witness the remarkable management methods devised at Minsmere that have made it the most famed of all the RSPB's seventy reserves.

The appointment of Herbert Axell as Senior Warden in 1959 could not have been more fortunate because following the excitement of 1947 had come disappointment. By the very next year conditions had deteriorated for these most demanding of birds. Although eight of them returned in April, they moved on before the end of that month. Neither the water levels nor the supply of food met their special requirements. Happily at Havergate where conditions could be controlled with sluices, the avocets established a successful although fluctuating colony and within a few years reached one hundred pairs.

It was not until 1963 that they could be persuaded to return to Minsmere and establish a second regular colony. That they returned at all was largely thanks to Herbert's vision, determination and dedication. Above all, he seems to have the exceptional gift of putting himself in the place of the bird to work out its requirements.

Soon after arriving, he realised what was needed, and embarked on the immense task of supervising the clearing of a fifty-acre stretch of reedy meadowland to create a shallow lagoon with fifty or so islands to provide the right nesting conditions for a host of birds. By a system of sluices it is possible to control not only the depth of the water but also the salinity. This is all-important for avocets as it determines the availability of their food supply: the small crustaceans on which they live.

The whole area is known as the Scrape and apart from the avocets it has meant that 1,500 pairs of breeding birds have been added to the reserve. It was a herculean labour and represented an immense achievement in developing new management techniques.

A few years ago Minsmere was the subject of one of the RSPB's films *A Welcome in the Mud*. I was the reporter with Herbert Axell of course as the guide. The film was made in early spring, and the day before shooting began Anthony Clay, then in charge of the

film unit, and Alan Macgregor, the chief cameraman, visited the
reserve to fix the best camera positions and so on.

Unfortunately it was a late spring that year and we had to contend
with biting north-easters and driving rain. From time to time the
film camera with its heavy tripod had to be humped over dyke
walls. While giving a helping hand, Herbert slipped and tore a
ligament in his leg. A little later that day, my gumboots failed to
grip on a stretch of particularly slimy mud and I slithered at speed
down a bank to finish up to my waist in icy water. Luckily for me
Alan Macgregor is not only a brilliant cameraman but also full of
resource and he had a spare pair of trousers tucked away in his
Land-Rover for just such an emergency. Even so, by the time we
got back to base that evening we looked as if we'd been on the
retreat from Moscow.

Next day the weather was a little kinder but Herbert was limping
badly and in considerable pain. I was fighting off a cold as a result of
my ducking, but the show went on and somehow the film was
made.

Herbert's fame has since spread far and wide and, his job completed at Minsmere, he is now available in an advisory capacity for
other bird conservation projects. At the time of writing he will
shortly be visiting the famous Coto Doñana Sanctuary in southern
Spain at the behest of the Spanish Government.

On another occasion when Herbert was still at Minsmere, I
dropped in to see him at his bungalow one morning to find him
looking a little the worse for wear. It was early summer and the
islands on the Scrape were a mass of nesting birds. To make sure
they were not disturbed I knew that he had organised all-night
watches and had borrowed a portable searchlight, in the event of
marauders on a moonless night. He explained that he hadn't had
much sleep the previous night. While in the tiny guard hut he'd
heard panic cries from an island, where he knew there were twelve
nests of avocets and ten nests of little terns. He immediately switched
on the searchlight and could plainly see a fox. Apparently un-
concerned, it slunk over to a little tern's nest and proceeded to eat
the contents, while the wretched bird hovered helplessly overhead.

Herbert knew there was only one answer if he wasn't going to
lose his avocets as well. He tied a long electric torch securely to the

barrel of his shot-gun and moved out into the Scrape in the black-
ness and against the wind and rain. Fortunately he knew every inch
of the way through the mud and water. Reaching the edge of the
island, he suddenly switched on the light. The fox stood stock still
in the white glare, its eyes glinting. There was all the time in the
world to aim and Herbert made no mistake: a yelp, a splash and then
pandemonium as three thousand birds from all the islands took off –
screaming.

By daylight he found three pairs of avocets and three pairs of
terns had lost their eggs. If he hadn't put paid to that fox it would
have been back night after night and scarcely any young would have
survived. As it was, in that same season, the thirty-three pairs of
avocets were able to fledge sixty-five young.

He looked tired that morning, but happy.

Someone once said that the real success of a sanctuary depends
not on barbed wire but on hard, slogging work. True enough, but
on many other qualities besides. In his book on Minsmere, Herbert
describes finding a young avocet a few days old which had become
separated from its parents at a time of heavy flood. It was lying on a
bank of wet clay and appeared to be dead. He picked it up and
slipped it in his trouser pocket:

On reaching my cottage I found the body was warm and dry and, on
impulse, I placed the tiny beak into my mouth and blew gently and very
briefly into the nostrils. The body jerked internally in response and in case
this was no more than just a mechanical reaction it was placed on a saucer
on top of the warm kitchen stove. Gradually, at first with almost im-
perceptible movements of the chick's wings and legs, the spark of life
which had been remaining in the little body grew into a determined
struggle for survival. Within two hours its eyes had re-opened and it was
calling weakly. But it could not stand. Now, at sunset, it had to be decided
whether to keep the bird warm and dry indoors until first light on the next
day or whether to return it to a place on the mud as near as possible to its
family.

H. E. Axell and Eric Hosking: 'Minsmere, Portrait of a Bird Reserve'

Herbert decided the care of the parents would give the chick the
best chance of survival so back he went to the marsh, placed the
little warm body on the wet ground near the parents and waited.

Soon he saw one of the parent birds stop, as though listening to the chick's cheepings. It then flew over, inspected its offspring, and settled over it to brood. Five weeks later the young bird was safely on the wing.

It seems to me a fine thing that men like Herbert Axell can give of themselves year after year twenty-four hours a day, if need be, to watch over the birds in their care.

I would also go so far as to say that the immense and growing interest now shown by the general public in all natural life is one of the most exciting and positive developments in Britain since the war. The RSPB alone now numbers over a quarter of a million members and the figures increase daily.

Since retiring from BBC Television News nearly five years ago I have had many more opportunities for travel and have been round the world twice. Seen from afar, Britain may appear played out, torn with self-inflicted wounds, floundering in depression. And yet perhaps, in our muddled way, we are trying to show the world that there can be more to living than the unbridled pursuit of a materialist technology.

It is a lesson I know some of us have learnt from observing the age-old life of the birds. In the words of Christina Chapin:

> Some spring of love and trust, some sense of light,
> Some inner beauty that is theirs alone
> Flows still from Eden where their spirits dwell.

Acknowledgements

The author would like to express his gratitude for permission to quote from the following works:

JOHN BAKER (Publishers) LTD. Verse by John Hewitt from *The Animal Anthology* ed. by Diana Spearman.

BARRIE & JENKINS LTD. and MICHAEL JOSEPH LTD. 'Stormcock in Elder' by Ruth Pitter from *A Book of Comfort* by Elizabeth Goudge.

BARRIE & JENKINS LTD. *The Happy Countryman* by E. L. Roberts.

THE BODLEY HEAD LTD. *Birds Wild and Free* by A. W. P. Robertson.

WILLIAM COLLINS SONS & CO. LTD. *Birds as Individuals* by Len Howard.

WILLIAM COLLINS SONS & CO. LTD. Verse by Marie de la Welch from *The House Sparrow* by D. Sumners-Smith.

WILLIAM COLLINS SONS & CO. LTD. and A. D. PETERS & CO. LTD. 'A Prospect of Swans' from *Poems of Many Years* by Edmund Blunden.

J. M. DENT & SONS LTD. 'Starlings in Trafalgar Square' and 'The Swans' from *Collected Poems* by Clifford Dyment.

ANDRE DEUTSCH LTD. Verse from *My Many Coated Man* by Laurie Lee (London 1955).

FABER AND FABER LTD. *England's Birds* by W. K. Richmond.

FABER AND FABER LTD. 'Thrushes' from *Lupercal* by Ted Hughes.

VICTOR GOLLANCZ LTD. 'Swans Mating' from *An Exploded View, Poems 1968–72* by Michael Longley.

RUPERT HART-DAVIS/GRANADA PUBLISHING LTD. and MICHAEL JOSEPH LTD. 'A Blackbird Singing' by R. S. Thomas from *A Book of Comfort* by Elizabeth Goudge.

RUPERT HART-DAVIS/GRANADA PUBLISHING LTD. Verse by Catullus translated by James Michie.

A. M. HEATH & CO. LTD. and the Estate of the late Henry Williamson: *The Lone Swallow* by Henry Williamson.

HODDER & STOUGHTON LTD., A. P. WATT LTD. and the Estate of the late Lord Grey of Fallodon: *The Charm of Birds* by Lord Grey of Fallodon.

Acknowledgements

HOUGHTON MIFFLIN LTD. Verse by Jennie B. Rittenhouse from *A Bird-Lover's Anthology* by Clinton Scollard and Jennie B. Rittenhouse.

HURST & BLACKETT LTD. (imprint of HUTCHINSON PUBLISHING GROUP): *The Murmur of Wings* by Leonard Dubkin.

HUTCHINSON & CO. (PUBLISHERS) LTD. *Minsmere, Portrait of a Bird Reserve* by H. E. Axell and Eric Hosking.

MACMILLAN, London and Basingstoke, A. P. WATT LTD., M. B. Yeats and Miss Anne Yeats: 'The Wild Swans at Coole' from *The Collected Poems of W. B. Yeats*.

THE LITERARY TRUSTEES OF WALTER DE LA MARE and THE SOCIETY OF AUTHORS as their representative: 'Titmouse' and 'The Tomtit' from *Collected Poems* by Walter de la Mare.

METHUEN & CO. LTD. 'The Redbreast' by Anthony Rye from *An Animal Anthology* compiled by Fougasse (London 1957).

METHUEN & CO. LTD., A. P. WATT LTD. and the Estate of the late D. M. Stuart: *A Book of Birds and Beasts* by D. M. Stuart.

JONATHAN NEVILLE *The Swans* by Derek Neville

NEWCASTLE EVENING CHRONICLE: article on a Kestrel's nest by James Alder.

OXFORD UNIVERSITY PRESS LTD. 'The Great Brown Owl' by Aunt Effie (J. E. Browne) from *The Oxford Book of Children's Verse* ed. by Iona and Peter Opie.

MARTIN SECKER & WARBURG LTD. 'The Missel Thrush' and 'The Cuckoo' from *Complete Poems* by Andrew Young ed. by Leonard Clark.

MARTIN SECKER & WARBURG LTD. and DAVID HIGHAM ASSOCI-ATES LTD. *Poems and Pictures* by Ford Madox Ford (Hueffer).

SEELEY, SERVICE & COOPER LTD. *Oddities of Natural History* by Eric Parker.

SIDGWICK & JACKSON LTD. 'He Comes on Chosen Evenings' from *Collected Poems of John Drinkwater*.

H. F. & G. WITHERBY LTD. Verse by Christina Chapin from *The Bird Lover's Book of Verse* collected by Christina Chapin.

H. F. & G. WITHERBY LTD. *Early Annals of Ornithology* by J. H. Gurney.

YORKSHIRE POST: 'It Takes All Sorts' by Mrs Edith Simpson.

I would ask forgiveness from anyone whose rights I may have inadvertently overlooked.